Francine Prince's Quick and Easy Diet Gourmet Recipes

Delicious gourmet cuisine in as
little as 10 minutes!

No sugar, no salt, low fat, low cholesterol,
low calorie, high fiber, high in flavor!

Illustrations by Polly Pezzello

A FIRESIDE BOOK
PUBLISHED BY SIMON & SCHUSTER, INC.
NEW YORK

Copyright © 1983 by Diet for Life Productions, Inc.
Illustrations Copyright © 1983 Polly Pezzello
All rights reserved
including the right of reproduction
in whole or in part in any form
First Fireside Edition, 1986
Published by Simon & Schuster, Inc.
Simon & Schuster Building
Rockefeller Center
1230 Avenue of the Americas
New York, New York 10020

FIRESIDE and colophon are registered trademarks of Simon & Schuster, Inc.

Manufactured in the United States of America

10   9   8   7   6   5   4   3   2   1

Library of Congress Cataloging in Publication Data
Prince, Francine.
   Francine Prince's Quick and easy diet gourmet recipes.

   Includes index.
   1. Cookery for the sick.   I. Title.   II. Title: Quick
and easy diet gourmet recipes.
RM219.P73   1984   641.5′63   83-15308
ISBN: 0-671-63296-5

A note of caution:

The nutritional information in this book is based on the experiences of my husband and myself, and on our studies of the pertinent literature. It is not intended, nor should it be regarded, as medical advice. When contemplating a change of diet, it is advisable to seek the guidance of your physician.

Other books by Francine Prince:

THE DIETER'S GOURMET COOKBOOK
DIET FOR LIFE
FRANCINE PRINCE'S NEW GOURMET RECIPES FOR DIETERS
FRANCINE PRINCE'S VITAMIN DIET FOR QUICK AND EASY WEIGHT LOSS
THE BEST OF FRANCINE PRINCE'S DIET GOURMET RECIPES
FRANCINE PRINCE'S GOURMET RECIPES FOR DIABETICS

This book is dedicated with enormous affection to my remarkable husband, Harold, who tasted and retasted every recipe, and who has been my loving source of encouragement throughout the years-long development of my gourmet cuisine of health.

Contents

Make It
Fast-Faster-Fastest

You're out of the kitchen with a finished dish—
Or—
You're out of the kitchen while a dish cooks merrily along without you—
In just 20 minutes—with my *fast* recipes,
In just 15 minutes—with my *faster* recipes, and
In just 10 minutes—with my *fastest* recipes.

And every dish is the kind of culinary masterpiece food lovers have come to expect from my gourmet cuisine of health.

It's the only cuisine which eliminates, or reduces to acceptable minimums, *all* nutritional no-no's.

It contains no sugar and no salt. It's low in fat, saturated fat, and cholesterol. It's as stingy with calories as it's generous with flavor.

And there's an additional bonus: It's high in fiber.

Only on this healthful, mouth-watering cuisine can you reduce and stay reduced on fast foods.

And on faster foods.

And on the fastest gourmet diet foods ever.

The Gourmet Cuisine of Health

Using only healthful ingredients, I've created dishes of striking originality. They possess the basic qualities discerning gourmets applaud in food: exciting flavors, sweetness, creaminess, and the taste of fat. Here's how I've accomplished this without salt, sugar, cream, or excess fat.

For exciting flavors, I rely on new combinations of tangy spices, fresh and dried herbs and vegetables, as well as aromatic seeds. I never use a salt substitute. Salt provides just one kind of taste. My flavors are a cornucopia of taste sensations.

For sweetness, I use the following no-sugar products: fresh and cooked fruits; dried fruits; fresh and packaged fruit juices; frozen concentrated fruit juices; sweet spices, herbs, and vegetables; and sometimes honey. I also use occasionally two other interesting natural sweeteners: date sugar, which is not a sugar at all, but ground dried dates; and The Healthy Sweetener, a mixture of ground dried dates and toasted bran.

For creaminess, I select nonfat liquid milk and evaporated milk (which, beaten with my technique, makes the base for scrumptious low-calorie ice creams and other feather-light desserts and toppings).

For the taste of fat, I choose peanut oil, a mixture of peanut oil and Italian olive oil, sweet unsalted corn oil margarine, and Country Morning Blend—an amalgam of sweet unsalted margarine and butter, with the kind of buttery taste no margarine can match. (Country Morning Blend contains more polyunsaturated fat than butter; and that influenced my judgment, too, but any brand of sweet unsalted margarine-butter blend will do.)

But what sets this cuisine apart most of all are the innovations—the unexpected mix of ingredients—that transform the dull into the delectable.

Getting Ready

You don't have to be a whiz in the kitchen to prepare my fast-faster-fastest dishes. Just follow these simple aids to cutting kitchen time:

1. Stock up on bare basics. Chances are you have many of them in your kitchen right now. Check the list on page 181. But do begin today to make my Ready-Access Foods (pages 177 to 180) which include three original tongue-tingling herb-and-spice mixtures.

2. Check among your kitchen ware to be sure you have these eight basic utensils: a 10- to 12-inch nonstick skillet; an iron skillet, same size; a 1½- to 2-quart covered saucepan; an ovenproof casserole dish; a food blender; a whisk; a cutting board; a sharp knife and sharpening steel. You'll save more time when you add an electric mixer, a food processor, a pressure cooker, and a wok to your possessions.

3. Read the recipe you're about to prepare to get the feel of it. Look particularly for these guidelines: Your kitchen time—like TEN MINUTES; the major utensil(s) required—like USE NONSTICK SKILLET; and special instructions—like PREHEAT OVEN TO 400°F. Then assemble your ingredients in order of use (that's the order in which they appear in the recipe), select your utensils, follow the recipe—and go!

Why These Recipes Help You Diet

They're low in sodium. Sodium makes you retain water. When you slash your sodium intake, excess water in your body drains away—ten pounds of it in about two weeks.

They're low in fat. Fat contains more than twice the calories of equivalent amounts of carbohydrates and proteins. When you replace fat with those nutrients, you can increase the amount of food you eat and still take in less calories. It's a way of losing one to three pounds of body fat a week—on a full stomach.

They're high in fiber, which fills you up fast and prevents some of the food from passing through your digestive tract into the rest of your body. There's no sodium in fiber, and no calories.

They're free from appetite stimulants—salt, sugar, and excess fat—which can wreck any diet.

And—

They're healthful. This is the kind of diet, according to the Federal Dietary Guidelines, which helps prevent such nutrition-related diseases as heart attack, atherosclerosis, adult-onset diabetes, gout, high blood pressure, and hypoglycemia.

(The proper vitamin supplements can speed up any reducing program. If you're interested in discovering just how, refer to my *Vitamin Diet for Quick and Easy Weight Loss*.)

At the bottom of each recipe, you'll find the calorie count and the sodium count (in milligrams) per serving.

Don't let your sodium intake exceed 1,000 milligrams a day while reducing, and 1,000 to 3,000 milligrams a day while holding your weight steady.

When you're reducing to your ideal weight (see the following charts), it's a good idea to calculate your daily caloric intake as follows:

Multiply your ideal weight by 10 if you lead an inactive life; by 15 if you lead a moderately active life; and by 20 if you lead a very active life. Then, if your age is 25 to 34, subtract 0; 35 to 44, subtract 100; 45 to 54, subtract 200; and 55 to 59, subtract 300.

When you've reached your ideal weight, continue with the same amount of calories each day (by that time your body will be happy with the reduced caloric intake)—and your weight will remain rock steady as long as you live.

Final Bonus

This is not "diet" cuisine in the ordinary sense of the word. It's not diet-y, it's not boring, it's not ugh-ly. It's not even remotely restrictive—it actually expands the joys of the table. It's a cuisine you can serve to anybody, even the boss's wife or your mother-in-law—and get standing ovations time after time. And it's a cuisine you and your family can enjoy for the rest of your life.

Good eating and good health!

Ideal Weight Tables

WOMEN

Height (without shoes)	Weight (without clothing)		
	SMALL FRAME	MEDIUM FRAME	LARGE FRAME
4'9"	99—108	103—118	115—128
4'10"	100—110	108—120	117—131
4'11"	101—112	100—123	119—134
5'0"	103—115	113—126	122—137
5'1"	105—118	115—129	125—140
5'2"	108—121	118—132	128—144
5'3"	111—124	121—135	131—148
5'4"	114—127	124—138	134—152
5'5"	117—130	127—141	137—156
5'6"	120—133	130—144	140—160
5'7"	123—136	133—147	143—164
5'8"	126—139	136—150	146—167
5'9"	129—142	139—153	149—170
5'10"	132—145	142—166	152—173
5'11"	135—148	145—159	155—176

MEN

Height (without shoes)	Weight (without clothing)		
	SMALL FRAME	MEDIUM FRAME	LARGE FRAME
5'1"	123—129	126—136	133—145
5'2"	125—131	128—138	135—148
5'3"	127—133	130—140	137—151
5'4"	129—135	132—143	139—155
5'5"	131—137	134—146	143—159
5'6"	133—140	137—149	144—163
5'7"	135—143	140—152	147—167
5'8"	137—146	143—155	150—171
5'9"	139—149	146—158	153—175
5'10"	141—152	149—161	156—179
5'11"	144—155	152—165	159—183
6'0"	147—159	155—169	163—187
6'1"	150—163	159—173	167—192
6'2"	153—167	162—177	171—197
6'3"	157—171	166—182	176—202

Adapted from the 1983 Metropolitan Life Insurance Company Health and Safety Education Division's Height and Weight Tables based on lowest mortality for men and women 25 to 59.

Fastest Recipes

Barbequed Baby Lamb Chops (10 minutes)

Let me sing the praises of lamb. Red as beef, and with more pizazz, its flavorful flesh seems made to order for the creation of easy-to-make gastronomic pleasures. See for yourself, as you start with lean, tender rib chops, add an impertinent barbeque sauce (original, of course), quick-broil, then cry hallelujah! as you taste the morsels of this juicy, rose-pink delight. (Rose-pink? Cook lamb to the doneness you like, but for my taste, rare is right.)

Preheat broiler

3   tablespoons tomato puree (no salt added)
1   tablespoon Italian olive oil
2   tablespoons each apple juice (no sugar added) and fresh lemon juice
½   teaspoon prepared Dijon mustard (no salt added)

1½ teaspoons Barbeque Spice Mix (page 178)
1½ teaspoons minced dried onions
1   tablespoon minced parsley
8   baby lamb chops, cut from the rib (2¼ pounds)

1. Prepare barbeque sauce by combining all ingredients, except meat, in heavy-bottomed saucepan. Bring to simmering point. Stir to blend. Cover and simmer gently for 5 minutes. Mixture will reduce and thicken.

2. Wipe chops with paper toweling. Arrange on rack in shallow broiling pan. Spoon half of sauce onto chops. Broil 4 inches from heat for 7 minutes. Turn. Spoon with balance of sauce. Broil for 7 minutes. Chops will be medium-rare to medium, depending upon thickness. Serve immediately.

YIELD: Serves 4

NOTE: Sauce is excellent spread on pork or veal chops before cooking.

	CALORIES	SODIUM
Per serving:	249.5	98

Skillet Lamb Chops with White Wine
(10 minutes)

The delicate wine-and-shallot sauce, set apart from other sauces by citrus tanginess, creates a fragrant and delectable dish.

Use iron skillet

8   baby lamb chops, cut from the rib (2¼ pounds trimmed weight)
1½ teaspoons Herb 'n Spice Mix (page 177)
1   tablespoon sweet unsalted margarine-butter blend (page 182)
3   tablespoons minced shallots

½   teaspoon finely grated lemon rind
⅓   cup white wine or dry vermouth
1   teaspoon frozen orange juice concentrate (no sugar added)
2   tablespoons minced parsley, dill, or mint

1. Wipe chops dry with paper toweling. Sprinkle and rub on both sides with Herb 'n Spice Mix.

2. Heat margarine-butter blend in a well-seasoned iron skillet until melted and moderately hot. Add shallots and sauté for 1 minute. Then lay chops on mixture. Sauté over medium-high heat for 3 minutes on each side.

3. Sprinkle chops with lemon rind.

Add wine and orange juice concentrate, turning chops several times to coat. Bring to simmering point. Cook, uncovered, turning often until sauce is reduced by more than half and chops are medium-rare (about 5 minutes). Transfer to warmed individual plates. Spoon with remaining sauce. Sprinkle with fresh parsley, dill, or mint. Serve immediately.

YIELD: Serves 4

	CALORIES	SODIUM
Per serving:	248.5	91.5
With dill or mint	No appreciable difference	
With dry vermouth	No appreciable difference	

Roast Crusty Rack of Lamb (10 minutes)

My novel herb-and-spice breading, crisped while roasting, seals in the rich juices, the delectable flavor, and the fork-tenderness of this nonpareil cut of lamb.

Preheat oven to 425°F

¼ cup Onion Rye Loaf fine bread crumbs (page 174) or crumbs made from good quality commercial rye bread

1 teaspoon Herb 'n Spice Mix (page 177)

1 tablespoon minced parsley

½ teaspoon finely grated lemon rind

1 teaspoon each tomato paste (no salt added) and prepared Dijon mustard (no salt added)

1 tablespoon Italian olive oil

¼ cup dry red wine

1 tablespoon minced shallot

1 small (2¼ pounds) rack of lamb (8 rib chops, partially cut through), well trimmed

Watercress sprigs

1. In small bowl, combine and blend in listed order first 8 ingredients. Mixture will be thick.

2. Wipe meat with paper toweling (it must be bone dry). Spread pastelike mixture onto all surfaces, pushing some into precut spaces, and onto sides of both end chops. Let stand for at least 15 minutes.

3. Place meat on rack in shallow roasting pan, bone side down. Cover loosely with aluminum foil. Bake in center section of preheated oven for 20 minutes. Uncover and bake for 20 minutes. Meat will be medium rare. (Chop may be partially cut through to see if meat is done to your liking.)

4. Cut chops with very sharp knife, taking care to collect any broken pieces of crust and serve them alongside meat portions. Serve on heated plates, garnished with watercress sprigs.

YIELD: Serves 4

	CALORIES	SODIUM
Per serving:	262	96.5
With commercial rye bread crumbs	263	107.5

Sophisticated Lamb Steaks (10 minutes)

My husband tells me that long, long ago, where the Twin Towers now surge upward into the New York skyline, there stood a friendly row of bistros on a quiet side-street. In one of them Harold for the first time came face-to-plate with a lamb steak, and it was love at first bite. My mission impossible, should I choose to accept it, was to duplicate the taste of that once-in-a-lifetime experience, based only on his palate's memory of things past. I chose to accept it, and here's the result. I hope you're as ecstatic about it as Harold is. P.S. On a practical note: Lamb steaks are an economical expedient when it's inconvenient to buy a whole leg of lamb.

Preheat broiler

1   tablespoon fresh lime juice
1   tablespoon peanut oil or Italian olive oil
1   teaspoon wine vinegar
2   teaspoons each tomato paste (no salt added) and prepared Dijon mustard (no salt added)
1   teaspoon no-fat Sap Sago cheese (page 182)

½   teaspoon dried cilantro leaves, crumbled
1   teaspoon chili con carne seasoning (no salt or pepper added)
4   teaspoons minced fresh garlic
2   well-aged lamb steaks cut ½-inch thick (1½ pounds), well trimmed

1. Combine all ingredients except meat in dessert cup or small bowl. Blend with fork. Mixture will be consistency of thick paste.

2. Wipe meat with paper toweling. Spoon and spread equal amounts of mixture on both sides of lamb.

3. Arrange on rack in shallow broiling pan. Broil under medium-high heat for 4 minutes. Turn. Broil 4 minutes. Repeat broiling and turning procedure twice more. (Meat tastes best if it's not overcooked—overcooking destroys nutritional value by 50 percent.)

4. Cut each slice in half. Serve on hot plates immediately.

YIELD: Serves 4

SERVING SUGGESTION: Asparagus Vinaigrette (page 93) and Cardamom Potatoes (page 94) make fine accompaniments to this unusual dish.

	CALORIES	SODIUM
Per serving:	267.5	91
With Italian olive oil	No appreciable difference	

Elegant Pork Pizza (10 minutes)

A pizza is dough, topping, and sauce. But in my pizza, instead of the traditional dough sprinkled with oil and spread with mozzarella, I use a novel bread-crumb mix which combines barbeque spices (not oregano) with skim milk mozzarella. Instead of the thick familiar toppings (sausages, anchovies, salami, and so on) I innovate with delicate and tender fillets of pork. And instead of a tired, routine tomato sauce, I spoon on a sparklingly fresh counterpart created especially for this recipe. All of those "insteads" add up to—elegance.

Preheat broiler

4 lean boneless pork loin chops, cut ¾ inch thick (1 pound), well trimmed
2 tablespoons wine vinegar
½ teaspoon finely grated lemon rind
2 teaspoons minced dried onions
1 tablespoon olive oil (see Note, page 36)
2½ teaspoons Barbecue Spice Mix (page 178)

2 teaspoons tomato paste (no salt added)
⅓ cup Onion Rye Loaf soft bread crumbs (page 174) or soft crumbs from good quality thin-sliced commercial rye bread
3 tablespoons grated part-skim mozzarella cheese
2 tablespoons minced parsley

1. Wipe meat with paper toweling. In cup, combine and blend vinegar, lemon rind, dried onions, olive oil, 2 teaspoons Barbeque Spice Mix, and tomato paste. Mixture will be thick. Let stand while next step is completed.

2. In cup, combine bread crumbs, grated cheese, remaining ½ teaspoon Barbeque Spice Mix, and parsley. Set aside.

3. Arrange pork fillets on rack in broiling pan. Spread half of onion mixture over one side of fillets. Broil 4 to 5

inches from heat for 10 minutes. Spoon with pan juices. Turn. Spread balance of onion mixture over fillets. Broil for 10 minutes. Baste with pan juices.

4. Spoon meat with equal mounts of bread-cheese mixture, pressing into meat to hold. Baste again with pan juices. Return to broiler and broil for 5 minutes, or until cheese is melted and mixture is lightly browned. Serve at once.

YIELD: Serves 4

	CALORIES	SODIUM
Per serving:	290	145
With commercial rye bread crumbs	289	174

Heavenly Pork Sauté (10 minutes)

Only four short steps to heaven!

Use iron skillet

8 thin-cut boneless pork chops (1½ pounds), well trimmed (see Note)
2 teaspoons Barbeque Spice Mix (page 178)
4 teaspoons Italian olive oil

1 tablespoon minced garlic
½ cup dry red or white wine
½ teaspoon grated orange rind (preferably from navel orange)
2 sprigs parsley

1. Wipe chops dry with paper toweling. Sprinkle and rub on both sides with spice mix.

2. Spread 2 teaspoons oil across large well-seasoned iron skillet. Heat until hot over medium-high heat. Spread garlic across skillet. Cook for 30 seconds. Lay meat on garlic in one layer. Sauté until lightly browned on both sides (about 3 minutes), adding balance of oil (2 teaspoons) when turning.

3. Pour wine around meat. Add orange rind. Bring to simmering point. Spoon over meat, turning several times to coat. Push parsley sprigs into liquid. Cover and simmer for 20 minutes, turning once midway.

4. Transfer chops to hot individual serving plates. Cover to keep warm. Discard parsley. Turn up heat under skillet and reduce sauce to 4 tablespoons. Spoon over chops, and serve immediately.

YIELD: Serves 4

NOTE: In my market, I usually find boneless pork chops (or fillets) cut about ¾ inch thick. I buy four chops and slice them to just-right thickness.

VARIATIONS:

1. Add 2 large fresh mushrooms, minced, or 2 tablespoons Ready Duxelles (page 180) to skillet with garlic in step 2.

2. Reduce wine to ¼ cup and add ¼ cup Delicious Chicken Stock (page 162) and 2 teaspoons tomato paste (no salt added) in step 3. Continue with balance of recipe.

3. Substitute for pork 1½ pounds thin-sliced chicken breasts or boneless veal (cut from leg).

	CALORIES	SODIUM
Per serving:	319	103
With white wine	No appreciable difference	
With mushrooms, add	+3.5	+2
With duxelles, add	+3	+0.5
With Delicious Chicken Stock and tomato paste, add	+4.5	+8
With chicken breasts	238	105.5
With veal	274	157

Sumptuous Broiled Veal Chops (10 minutes)

How would you like to star in a real-life commercial that sells *you*, like so:

YOU: How do you like my veal chops?

NEIGHBOR: Mmmmmm. Good! Bet there's oodles of ingredients in them.

YOU: Only seven.

NEIGHBOR: Only *seven*! Ooooh, *de*-licious! Bet it takes an hour to prepare.

YOU: Only ten minutes.

NEIGHBOR: Only *ten* minutes! Bet you won't let me have the recipe—?

YOU: Sure I will.

NEIGHBOR: *Won*-derful! You're the greatest!

Hype? No. It happened to me. It can happen to you. Good recipes make good neighbors.

Preheat broiler

¼ cup sweet Marsala wine
3 tablespoons pineapple juice (no sugar added)
1½ teaspoons Indian Spice Mix (page 178)
1½ teaspoons tomato paste (no salt added)

1 teaspoon dry mustard
1 tablespoon minced parsley or dill, or a combination of both
4 loin or rib veal chops (1½ pounds), well trimmed

1. Combine all ingredients except meat in a cup. Beat with a fork to blend.

2. Wipe chops dry with paper toweling. Lay on plate. Spoon with wine-spice mixture on both sides, using all of mixture. Let stand for 5 minutes.

3. Arrange chops on rack in broiling pan. Broil 4 inches from heat for 8 minutes. Turn. Spoon with pan juices. Broil for 8 minutes. Turn and spoon with pan juices twice more at 3-minute intervals. (Cooking time will vary with thickness of chops.) Finished chops should be browned on the outside and delicately pink and moist inside.

YIELD: Serves 4

NOTE: A counter-top broiler *without* thermostat control for broiling does a fine job here.

	CALORIES	SODIUM
Per serving:	234	156
With rib chops	No appreciable difference	

Veal Patties with Madeira (10 minutes)

Bland to the point of neutrality, veal needs the magic of sauce to animate it with a personality of its own. Here I conjure up a saucy mélange based on pert vegetables (onions and duxelles), impudent spices (Dijon mustard and Worcestershire), and flippant wine (Malmsey Madeira) to transform plain-Jane veal patties into a brassy dish. Pure sauce-ery!

Use nonstick skillet

2   slices Delicate Textured Loaf (page 171) or fine quality commercial enriched white bread
2   teaspoons tomato paste (no salt added)
1   teaspoon prepared Dijon mustard (no salt added)
6   tablespoons sweet Madeira wine (Malmsey)

½   teaspoon Worcestershire sauce
2   teaspoons minced dried onions
1   teaspoon onion powder
1   pound extra-lean ground veal
1   tablespoon Ready Duxelles (page 180)
2   tablespoons minced parsley
2   teaspoons Italian olive oil

1. Tear bread into small pieces and place in a bowl. In a cup, combine and blend tomato paste, mustard, 4 tablespoons wine, Worcestershire sauce, onions, and onion powder. Pour over bread and mash. Let stand for 2 minutes.

2. Add meat to mixture, blending well. Then work in balance of ingredients except oil. Shape into eight ½-inch-thick patties.

3. Heat oil in a nonstick skillet until hot. Sauté patties over medium-high heat on each side until lightly browned (about 5 minutes). Add balance of wine to skillet (2 tablespoons) and quickly spoon over patties. Serve immediately.

YIELD: Serves 4

	CALORIES	SODIUM
Per serving:	220	117
With commercial white bread	217.5	171.5

Filet Mignon Roast (10 minutes)

Most cuts of beef designated by supermarket labeling as "roast" are risky buys. You don't know whether they'll be savory or insipid, tender or tough. Not so with filet mignon. Select the less expensive choice cut (less fat and cholesterol), and you'll get a melt-in-the-mouth, full beef-flavored delight every time. Instruct your butcher to roll and tie it; then roast to perfection, spooning several times with my garlic-and-mustard sauce. You've never tasted another roast beef like it!

Preheat oven to 400°F

½ teaspoon each dried savory and tarragon leaves, crushed
¼ cup dry red wine
1 teaspoon prepared Dijon mustard (no salt added)
6 dashes ground red (cayenne) pepper

1 tablespoon minced garlic
1 tablespoon minced parsley
1½ pounds filet mignon roast, well-trimmed, rolled and tied to 3-inch diameter

1. Prepare basting mixture by combining all ingredients except meat in a bowl. Set aside.

2. Wipe meat. Place on rack in shallow roasting pan. Roast uncovered in preheated oven for 10 minutes. Spoon with basting mixture. Return to oven and roast 10 minutes. Turn. Repeat basting and turning sequence twice more. Meat will be medium rare in 40 minutes. Cook an additional 10 minutes for medium, if you prefer. (Do not overcook. Overcooking destroys nutritive value by 50 percent.)

3. With a sharp knife or electric knife, cut roast into ½-inch slices and serve immediately.

YIELD: Serves 4

VARIATION: Spoon with Delicate Wine Sauce (page 154)—a natural for this dish. The entire sauce may be prepared in 10 minutes!

	CALORIES	SODIUM
Per serving:	271	125.5
With Delicate Wine Sauce		
Per tablespoon, add	+8.5	+6.5
Per tablespoon, with milk, add	+10	+9

Spiced Beefburgers (10 minutes)

The gourmet's hamburgers. Surprise touch: bean sprouts for an exciting textural variation.

Use iron skillet

2   slices Delicate Textured Loaf (page 171), or 2 thin slices fine quality commercial enriched white bread or rye bread
3   tablespoons apple juice (no sugar added)
1   tablespoon evaporated skim milk
1   teaspoon tomato paste (no salt added)

1   pound extra-lean ground beef
1   teaspoon Herb 'n Spice Mix (page 177)
½   teaspoon ground cinnamon
⅓   cup well-drained and dried bean sprouts, coarsely chopped
2   tablespoons minced fresh dill
1   tablespoon peanut oil
2   tablespoons minced shallots

1. Tear bread into small pieces and place in a bowl. In a cup, combine and blend apple juice, skim milk, and tomato paste. Pour over bread and mash.

2. Add meat and spices to bread mixture, blending with fingers. Then add bean sprouts and dill, combining well. Shape into eight ½-inch-thick burgers.

3. Heat oil in a well-seasoned iron skillet until hot. Spread shallots across skillet. Sauté for 30 seconds. Lay burgers on shallots. Sauté over medium-high heat on each side for 3 minutes. Burgers should be browned on the outside and pink inside. Do not overcook. Serve immediately.

YIELD: Serves 4

VARIATIONS:

1. Substitute equal amount of Delicious Chicken Stock (page 162) for apple juice.

2. Prepare Spiced Beefballs: Shape meat into 16 meat balls. Following step 3, brown balls for about 3 minutes. Pour ⅓ cup dry red wine around meat. Bring to a boil, spooning several times over meat. Cover and simmer for 10 minutes, turning and spooning with wine once midway. Serve on warmed individual plates spooned with wine sauce.

	CALORIES	SODIUM
Per serving:	237.5	87
With commercial white bread	235	141.5
With commercial rye bread	229.5	147
With Delicious Chicken Stock	234.5	90
With ⅓ cup red wine	244	89

Faster Recipes

Exotic Lamb Meatballs (15 minutes)

My style of cooking is characterized by a balanced mixture of the fresh and original with a comfortable sense of the familiar. Take these plump, savory meatballs, for example. They're as exotic as tidbits from the kitchens of Kashmir, but at the same time they're as homespun as country cooking. Here's a no-risk-to-the-palate way to go gastronomic adventuring.

Use nonstick skillet

1 pound lean ground lamb	1 egg (use ½ egg yolk, all egg white), lightly beaten
1½ teaspoons Indian Spice Mix (page 178)	4 teaspoons tomato paste (no salt added)
¼ cup minced shallots	2 tablespoons unbleached flour
2 slices Onion Rye Bread (page 174) or good quality commercial rye bread, crusts trimmed	1 tablespoon Italian olive oil
1 tablespoon plus ⅓ cup Madeira wine (Malmsey)	⅔ cup Delicious Chicken Stock (page 162)
2 tablespoons evaporated milk	2 sprigs parsley

1. In bowl, combine meat, spice mix, and shallots, blending well.

2. Tear bread into small pieces and soak in 1 tablespoon Madeira and milk until well moistened. Add to meat and combine.

3. Beat egg with 2 teaspoons tomato paste. Add to meat and blend (your fingers will do the best job here). With moist hands, shape meat into 12 balls.

4. Sprinkle flour onto sheet of waxed paper. Roll balls in flour; then toss from one hand to another to evenly coat.

5. Heat oil in nonstick skillet until quite hot. Brown balls on all sides.

6. Combine chicken stock with ⅓ cup Madeira, and remaining 2 teaspoons tomato paste. Pour around meat. Add parsley sprigs. Bring to simmering point. Carefully turn balls to coat. Reduce heat. Cover and simmer for 20 minutes, turning and spooning with sauce once midway. Spoon with sauce again. Discard parsley sprigs. Remove from heat and let stand, covered, for 5 minutes. Sauce will thicken naturally.

YIELD: Serves 4

NOTE: The degree of deliciousness depends largely on the quality and leanness of the lamb. One way to get the right kind of ground lamb is to cut off one or two pounds of steaks when you buy a leg of lamb, freeze them, then when you're ready to use them, partially defrost, cut into 1-inch cubes, and grind the meat in your food processor, or grinder.

	CALORIES	SODIUM
Per serving:	254.5	117.5
With commercial rye bread	250	156.5

Succulent Pork Chops with Cranberries
(15 minutes)

Run your eyes down Chinese menus, and you'll need a computer to tote up the varieties of pork dishes. Pork—tender and pleasant tasting—has the kind of personality that gets along with, and brings out the best in, any food. Here, I borrow the Chinese concept of mingling this versatile meat with a surprising fruit to create a truly American combination—pork with cranberries. You'll find it as exciting as it is enterprising.

Use iron skillet

8   thin-sliced extra-lean loin pork chops (about 1¾ pounds), well trimmed
1½   teaspoons Barbeque Spice Mix (page 178)
1   tablespoon Italian olive oil
1   tablespoon minced fresh garlic

3   tablespoons each minced celery and sweet green pepper
⅓   cup each Delicious Chicken Stock (page 162) and grape juice (no sugar added)
½   cup fresh cranberries

1. Wipe chops with paper toweling. Sprinkle and rub on both sides with Barbeque Spice Mix.
2. Heat oil in large well-seasoned iron skillet until moderately hot. Spread garlic, celery, and green pepper across skillet. Sauté for 1 minute. Lay chops atop mixture. Lightly brown on both sides (about 4 minutes).

3. Add stock and grape juice. Bring to a boil. Add cranberries, pushing down into liquid. Bring to simmering point. Spoon with sauce. Cover tightly and simmer for 35 minutes, turning and spooning with sauce twice at equal intervals.

YIELD: Serves 2

SERVING SUGGESTIONS: Just-boiled peeled red-skinned potatoes, spooned with sauce, and New Coleslaw (page 131) or Red Cabbage Slaw (page 132) make excellent companions to this simple-to-make dish.

	CALORIES	SODIUM
Per serving:	257	66
Per potato	86	3

Luscious Rosemary Pork Chops (15 minutes)

Rosemary, so herbalists assert, bestows on you the gift of flawless memory. Whether you agree or not, one thing is certain: A dish seasoned discretely with this pungent and assertive shrub of the mint family is unforgettable. Here "discretely" means that rosemary is just one seasoning, albeit the dominant one, in a medley of palate-tingling herbs, juices, and spices.

Use iron skillet

4   loin pork chops cut ½ inch thick (1¾ pounds), well trimmed
2   teaspoons dried rosemary leaves, crushed
½   teaspoon ground ginger
2   teaspoons each peanut oil and Italian olive oil, combined
1   medium onion, minced
2   teaspoons minced garlic

3   large fresh mushrooms, rinsed, dried, trimmed, and coarsely chopped
1   tablespoon wine vinegar
¼   cup each apple juice (no sugar added) and tomato juice (no salt added)
2   tablespoons minced parsley

1. Wipe chops dry with paper toweling. Sprinkle and rub on both sides with 1 teaspoon rosemary and all of ginger.

2. Heat 2 teaspoons combined oil in well-seasoned iron skillet until hot. Add chops and brown lightly on both sides over medium heat. Transfer to plate.

3. Heat balance of oils (2 teaspoons). Sauté onion, garlic, and mushrooms for 2 minutes, stirring constantly. Add wine vinegar. Stir and cook for 30 seconds. Add apple juice, tomato juice, and parsley. Bring to simmering point.

4. Return browned chops to skillet, turning several times to coat. Cover and simmer for 35 minutes, turning and spooning with sauce twice at equal intervals. Uncover and cook over medium heat, turning often, until sauce is reduced to 4 tablespoons.

5. Serve on warmed individual plates, spooned with thickened sauce.

YIELD: Serves 4

SERVING SUGGESTION: Broccoli with Sesame Seed (page 106) or Bright Green Peas with Orange-Hued Pimentos (page 104) are fine companions to this dish.

	CALORIES	SODIUM
Per serving:	269.5	67

Veal Chops Supreme (15 minutes)

This is more sumptuous than my 10-minute Sumptuous Broiled Veal Chops (page 22), and worth every one of the additional 5 minutes it takes to prepare Special treat: the unusual mixture of seasonings.

Use nonstick skillet

2 tablespoons unbleached flour
2½ teaspoons Barbeque Spice Mix (page 178)
4 loin or rib veal chops cut ½-inch thick (1½ pounds), well trimmed
3 teaspoons Italian olive oil

1 tablespoon minced garlic
2 tablespoons minced sweet red pepper
¼ teaspoon finely grated lemon rind
¼ cup each apple juice (no sugar added) and dry red wine

1. In cup, combine flour with Barbeque Spice Mix. Wipe chops dry with paper toweling. Sprinkle and rub meat on both sides with flour mixture. (There will be enough for a light coating.)

2. Heat 2 teaspoons oil in nonstick skillet until quite hot. Spread garlic and sweet red pepper across skillet. Sprinkle with lemon rind. Sauté for 30 seconds. Lay chops on mixture. Sauté until well browned on both sides, adding balance of oil (1 teaspoon) after turning.

3. Pour apple juice and wine around sides of skillet. When liquid simmers, spoon over meat. Reduce heat to simmering. Cover and simmer for 30 minutes, turning twice and spooning with sauce at equal intervals.

4. Serve on warmed individual serving plates, spooned with sauce.

YIELD: Serves 4

	CALORIES	SODIUM
Per serving:	279.5	99
With rib chops	274	99

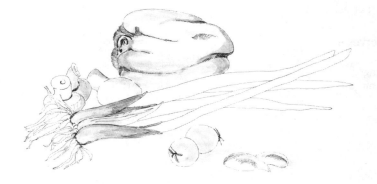

Veal Scallopini with Hearts of Artichokes
(15 minutes)

This is my version of a dish featured in one of New York's outstanding Italian restaurants. It exemplifies my practice of wedding ethnic traditions to healthful innovations to produce extravaganzas that delight the most diet-conscious gastronome.

Use nonstick skillet

1 9-ounce box frozen artichoke hearts
1 pound veal scallops, ¼ inch thick, cut from the leg
2 teaspoons Herb 'n Spice Mix (page 177)
2 tablespoons cornstarch

4 teaspoons Italian olive oil, or 2 teaspoons each peanut oil and Italian olive oil
¼ cup minced shallots
1 tablespoon tarragon vinegar
½ cup Marsala wine

1. Cook artichokes in rapidly boiling water for 1 minute. Drain. Cut each artichoke into quarters. Set aside.

2. Dry meat thoroughly with paper toweling. Lay on sheet of waxed paper in one layer. Combine Herb 'n Spice Mix with cornstarch. Sprinkle and rub half of mixture over each side of meat.

3. Heat half of oil in nonstick skillet until hot. Sauté half of meat on each side until delicately brown (about 1½ minutes total time). Transfer meat to plate. Add balance of oil to skillet and repeat process. Transfer second batch to plate. Set aside.

4. Add shallots and artichokes to skillet. Sauté over medium heat, stirring constantly for 2 minutes. Stir in tarragon vinegar. Cook for 30 seconds. Then add wine.

5. Return veal to skillet. Spoon with simmering sauce. Simmer, uncovered, for 3 minutes. (Most of liquid will be absorbed.)

6. Arrange scallopini on warmed individual plates surrounded by artichokes.

YIELD: Serves 4

Per serving:
With peanut oil

	CALORIES	SODIUM
	238	138
	No appreciable difference	

Three-Way Veal Stew with Apricots (15 minutes)

From the Middle East comes the inspiration for this unusual stew. There, apricots are the traditional complements of lamb in many cookpots. Here, veal replaces lamb to create a delicate, elegant stew with a soak-up-the-last-drop irresistibility (that's why I recommend serving it on a bed of rice). Try it *au naturel*, lightly thickened, or creamily textured with another gift from the lands east of Suez—yogurt.

Use pressure cooker

16 medium dried apricot halves
1 pound lean stewing veal, well trimmed, cut into 1-inch chunks
1 tablespoon Indian Spice Mix (page 178)
4 teaspoons Italian olive oil or peanut oil, or a combination of both
2 tablespoons minced celery
½ sweet green pepper, julienned
1 tablespoon minced garlic

¼ pound fresh mushrooms, washed, dried, trimmed, and thickly sliced
½ cup Delicious Chicken Stock (page 162)
¼ cup dry sherry
1 teaspoon finely grated lemon rind
1 tablespoon minced dried onions
3 sprigs parsley, wrapped into a neat bundle and tied with white thread

1. Place apricots in small bowl. Cover with water. Set aside.

2. Wipe meat thoroughly with paper toweling. Sprinkle with Indian Spice Mix.

3. Heat oil in pressure cooker until hot. Add meat, celery, green pepper, and garlic. Sauté until meat loses its pink color (about 4 minutes), turning every 30 seconds. Add mushrooms and sauté for 2 minutes.

4. Add balance of ingredients. Bring to simmering point. Close cover securely. Place regulator on vent pipe and cook for 25 minutes, with pressure regulator rocking slowly. Cool immediately under cold running water.

5. Discard parsley sprigs and serve over a bed of just-cooked rice (no salt added), allowing one-third cup per portion.

YIELD: Serves 4

VARIATIONS:

1. Thicken, if desired, with 1 tablespoon arrowroot flour dissolved in 1 tablespoon cold water, adding just enough to thicken lightly.

2. Stir in ½ cup room-temperature low-fat plain yogurt just before serving.

	CALORIES	SODIUM
Per serving (without rice):	192.5	128
With arrowroot flour	200	129
With low-fat plain yogurt	208.5	148
With ⅓ cup just-cooked rice, add	+77	+0

Osso Buco, My Style (15 minutes)

A spin-off on the Milanese version of this perennial Italian favorite (no carrots, celery, or tomato paste), my style osso buco replaces onions with shallots, white wine with sweet Madeira, butter with peanut oil, and lemon rind with orange juice. I also add, as no cook in Milan or throughout Italy has ever done, mushrooms, raisins, and my own chicken stock. The finished concoction is a tender, butternut-brown spiced veal shank, enriched by a contrasting sweet-wine-and-fruit sauce. Prepare this osso buco a day ahead (it's even better the following day), and luxuriate in leisure at your next dinner party.

Use Dutch oven

8   slices veal shank cut ½ inch thick (about 2½ pounds), well trimmed
2   tablespoons unbleached flour
2   teaspoons Barbeque Spice Mix (page 178)
2½ teaspoons each Italian olive oil and peanut oil
1   tablespoon minced garlic
3   tablespoons minced shallots

¼   pound fresh mushrooms, rinsed, dried, trimmed, and coarsely chopped
½   cup each Delicious Chicken Stock (page 162), fresh orange juice, and sweet Madeira wine (Malmsey)
¼   cup raisins
3   large sprigs parsley

1. Wipe meat dry with paper toweling. Combine flour with spice mix. Spread half of mixture on sheet of waxed paper. Press meat into mixture. Sprinkle meat with balance of spice mixture, pressing evenly into meat.

2. Heat 3 teaspoons oil in Dutch oven until hot. Lightly brown meat on both sides over medium-high heat (about 6 minutes), taking care not to scorch. Transfer to plate.

3. Spread balance of oil (2 teaspoons) across pot (it will heat rapidly). Sauté without browning, garlic, shallots, and mushrooms, stirring constantly until mixture begins to soften (about 3 minutes).

4. Add balance of ingredients. Bring to simmering point. Return meat to pot, turning several times to coat. Cover tightly. Reduce heat to simmering, and simmer for 40 minutes, turning and spooning with sauce 3 times at equal intervals.

5. Transfer meat to warmed serving dish. Cover to keep warm. Discard parsley sprigs. Turn up heat under Dutch oven and reduce sauce by a third. Spoon over meat and serve.

YIELD: Serves 4 or 5

NOTE: If prepared a day ahead, reheat in a nonstick skillet.

VARIATION: Substitute Indian Spice Mix (page 178) for Barbeque Spice Mix. A whole new flavor!

	CALORIES	SODIUM
Per serving, serves 4:	324	154.5
Per serving, serves 5:	259	123.5
With Indian Spice Mix	No appreciable difference	

Serendipity Steak (15 minutes)

Princess Serendipity, as every devoted follower of fairy-tale royalty knows, was blessed by the little folk with a rare gift. It was this: Whenever she went on a search for something, she never found it—she found something better. So Princess Serendipity, hunting for a diamond for her ring, stumbled on Aladdin's treasure trove instead. Which brings me to my point. I was looking in my cupboard for familiar ingredients with which to make a favorite steak, but I came away with a far more precious cargo of culinary gems instead. Hence, "Serendipity Steak."

Use iron skillet

1   pound (8 slices) filet mignon, ½ inch thick, well trimmed
1   teaspoon dried savory leaves, crushed
½   teaspoon chili con carne seasoning (no salt or pepper added)
2   teaspoons Italian olive oil
1   tablespoon wine vinegar
½   cup dry red wine
1   tablespoon tomato paste (no salt added)

1   teaspoon prepared Dijon mustard (no salt added)
2   teaspoons minced garlic
1   teaspoon peeled and minced fresh ginger
2   large fresh mushrooms, washed, dried, trimmed, and minced
1   tablespoon minced parsley

1. Wipe meat with paper toweling. Sprinkle and rub with savory and chili con carne seasoning.

2. Heat oil in well-seasoned iron skillet until hot. Sauté steaks for about 3 minutes on each side (medium rare). Do not overcook. Transfer to hot plate. Cover to keep warm.

3. Add wine vinegar to skillet. Deglaze for 30 seconds.

4. Combine wine with tomato paste and mustard. Add to skillet. Bring to a boil. Stir in remaining ingredients. Cook over medium-high heat for about 3 minutes. Finished sauce should be thick and spoonable.

5. Serve 2 slices of meat per portion on individual warmed serving plates. Spoon with sauce and serve immediately.

YIELD: Serves 4

	CALORIES	SODIUM
Per serving:	213	82

Filet Mignon in Mushroom-Orange Sauce
(15 minutes)

Warning: Try it, and you may never enjoy an ordinary broiled steak again.

Use iron skillet

1   pound (8 slices) filet mignon, ½ inch thick, well trimmed
2   teaspoons Barbeque Spice Mix (page 178)
2   teaspoons Italian olive oil
2   teaspoons sweet unsalted margarine-butter blend (page 182)
3   tablespoons minced shallots
2   tablespoons minced sweet red pepper

2   tablespoons white wine vinegar
4   teaspoons orange juice concentrate (no sugar added)
¼   cup Delicious Chicken Stock (page 162)
¼   pound fresh mushrooms, washed, dried, trimmed, and sliced

1. Wipe meat with paper toweling. Sprinkle and rub with Barbeque Spice Mix.

2. Heat oil in well-seasoned iron skillet until hot. Sauté steaks for about 3 minutes on each side (medium rare). Do not overcook. Transfer to plate. Cover to keep warm.

3. Heat 1 teaspoon margarine-butter blend in skillet, tilting pan from side to side to spread across evenly. Add shallots and sweet red pepper. Sauté for 2 minutes, or until lightly browned, stirring constantly.

4. Add white wine vinegar, and cook for 30 seconds. Stir in orange juice concentrate and stock. Bring to a boil.

5. Add mushrooms. Bring to a boil again. Cook over medium-high heat until sauce is reduced to thick consistency (about 3 minutes).

6. Swirl in remaining margarine-butter blend (1 teaspoon). Serve 2 slices of meat per portion in individual warmed serving plates. Spoon with sauce, and enjoy immediately.

YIELD: Serves 4

	CALORIES	SODIUM
Per serving:	240	89.5

Record-Fast Beef Stew (15 minutes)

It's also richer tasting than the beef-stew recipes you've used before. The secret is I don't cook the stew with carrots and onions, because they're flavor diluters if there ever were ones. Instead, I separately steam beef-compatible vegetables—carrots, potatoes, and green beans—and serve them on the side as-is or glossed with a soupçon of margarine or margarine-butter blend, and sprinkled with fresh herbs. Hint: Cook a pot of stew and freeze leftovers in heat-sealed boilable plastic bags for an almost-instant dish for some later day.

Use pressure cooker

2   pounds lean beef such as top or bottom round, cut into 1-inch cubes
2   teaspoons Indian Spice Mix (page 178)
1   tablespoon peanut oil or Italian olive oil
1   tablespoon minced garlic
1   small sweet green pepper, coarsely chopped

1   cup canned tomatoes (no salt added), chopped
1   tablespoon tomato paste (no salt added)
½   cup dry red wine
2   tablespoons dehydrated onion flakes
2   sprigs parsley

1. Wipe meat with paper toweling. Lay on sheet of waxed paper. Sprinkle with Indian Spice Mix. Turn meat chunks over several times until coated with spice mixture.

2. Heat oil in pressure cooker until hot. Sear meat on all sides (about 3 minutes), sprinkling any residue spice mix on waxed paper over meat. Then add garlic and green pepper. Stir and sauté for 1 minute.

3. Stir in balance of ingredients. Bring to simmering point. Cover pot securely. Place pressure regulator on vent pipe, and cook for 15 minutes, with pressure regulator rocking slowly. Cool at once under cold running water.

YIELD: Serves 6

VARIATIONS:

1. Add ¼ pound cleaned, trimmed, and thickly sliced snow-white fresh mushrooms and sauté with garlic and green pepper in step 2.

2. Thicken sauce by dissolving 1 tablespoon arrowroot flour in 1 tablespoon water. Bring cooked stew to simmering point. Dribble in only enough of mixture to slightly thicken sauce.

	CALORIES	SODIUM
Per serving:	249	103
With Italian olive oil	No appreciable difference	
With mushrooms	254	106
With arrowroot flour	254	104

Meat Loaf Muffins (15 minutes)

When is a meat loaf a muffin? When an adventurous mixture of ground lean beef and veal, bread crumbs, and wine are baked in muffin cups. Special bonus: Superb, too, when sliced and served cold next day.

Use nonstick skillet
Preheat oven to 425°F

½ pound each ground lean beef and veal
1½ teaspoons Herb 'n Spice Mix (page 177)
½ teaspoon ground cinnamon
3 tablespoons minced parsley or dill, or a combination of both
¼ cup Mixed Wheat Bread Crumbs (page 171) or bread crumbs made from good quality commercial whole-wheat bread
1 egg white

3 tablespoons Marsala wine
2 teaspoons Italian olive oil (see Note)
1 tablespoon minced garlic
4 large fresh mushrooms, washed, dried, trimmed, and minced, or 2 tablespoons Ready Duxelles (page 180)
2 tablespoons low-fat plain yogurt
½ teaspoon sweet unsalted corn oil margarine

1. Combine and blend meat with Herb 'n Spice Mix, cinnamon, parsley, and bread crumbs. Then blend in egg white which has been lightly beaten with fork, and Marsala.

2. Heat oil in nonstick skillet until hot. Sauté garlic and mushrooms for 3 minutes, turning constantly (do not brown). Add meat mixture. Blend well. Then blend in yogurt. (Your fingers will do the best job here.)

3. Shape into 4 equal balls. Place in margarine-greased Pyrex ¾ cup muffin dishes, or decorative ¾-inch molds. Place dishes on baking sheet. Bake in center section of preheated oven for 30 minutes.

4. Pour off any exuded fat from dishes. Place on warmed individual serving plates and serve *au naturel* (meat muffins will be moist and juicy).

YIELD: Serves 4

NOTE: For extraordinary flavor, use French or Italian olive oil designated "extra virgin."

SERVING SUGGESTION: Serve with Delicate Wine Sauce or Quick Mushroom Sauce (pages 154 and 156).

	CALORIES	SODIUM
Per serving:	232	128
With dill	No appreciable difference	
With Ready Duxelles	230	125

Fast Recipe

Fresh Ham with Mushrooms (20 minutes)

An utterly new way to prepare an old favorite.

Use iron skillet

1   pound thin-cut fresh ham, pounded to ¼-inch thickness
2½ teaspoons Barbeque Spice Mix (page 178)
1   tablespoon peanut oil
1   leek, white part only, minced
1   teaspoon minced garlic (optional)
¼   pound fresh mushrooms, washed, dried, trimmed and coarsely chopped

⅓   cup each dry white wine and pineapple juice (no sugar added)
1   teaspoon prepared Dijon mustard (no salt added)
½   cup loosely packed mint leaves, coarsely chopped
     Orange slices

1. Wipe meat dry with paper toweling. Sprinkle and rub 2 teaspoons Barbeque Spice Mix on both sides.

2. Heat oil in well-seasoned iron skillet until hot. Sauté meat on each side for 2 minutes. Transfer to plate.

3. Add leek, garlic, and mushrooms to skillet. Sauté for 2 minutes, stirring often (do not brown).

4. Stir in wine. Cook for 1 minute.

5. Add mustard and mint leaves. Bring to simmering point. Return meat to skillet, turning several times to coat. Cover tightly and simmer for 25 to 30 minutes, turning and spooning with sauce twice at equal intervals. Sauce will reduce and become thick.

6. Serve on warmed individual plates garnished with orange slices.

YIELD: Serves 4

SERVING SUGGESTION: Simple baked yams and a green salad make excellent accompaniments to this dish. See pages 129 to 137 for salad suggestions.

VARIATION: Add 3 tablespoons Delicious Chicken Stock (page 162) in step 4 for an extraordinarily rich-tasting sauce.

	CALORIES	SODIUM
Per serving:	341	86.5
With Delicious Chicken Stock	342	91

Chicken, Cornish Hens, and Turkey

Fastest Recipes

Lively Chicken Breasts (10 minutes)

Bill Bertenshaw, one of our favorite people, is the radio and TV director of The Council of Churches of the City of New York. When I served him this chicken dish at one of our dinner parties, he groaned, "I should have told you—all those church suppers have made me so bored with chicken, I can't even look at it." But properly coaxed and cajoled, he put fork to mouth. Grinned Bill, "This chicken's so lively, it doesn't even taste like chicken," and ate the whole thing. Moral: To snap anybody out of chicken boredom, wake up the chicken.

Use nonstick skillet

1½ pounds boned and skinned chicken breasts, ¼ inch thick

2 teaspoons Indian Spice Mix (page 178)

3 teaspoons Italian olive oil

1 tablespoon minced fresh garlic

1 large scallion, including tender green part, trimmed and thinly sliced

2 tablespoons minced sweet red pepper

¼ cup each dry vermouth and pineapple juice (no sugar added)

1 tablespoon minced parsley or dill

1. Wash chicken. Dry thoroughly with paper toweling. Sprinkle and rub on both sides with spice mix.

2. Heat 2 teaspoons oil in nonstick skillet until hot. Add chicken and lightly brown on both sides. Do not overcook. Transfer to a dish.

3. Add remaining teaspoon of oil. Sauté garlic, scallion, and sweet red pepper until lightly browned, stirring often (about 3 minutes). Return chicken to skillet, turning several times to coat.

4. Pour vermouth and pineapple juice around sides of skillet. Bring to simmering point. Spoon over chicken. Cover and simmer gently for 12 minutes, turning once midway. Uncover.

Turn up heat. Cook until sauce is reduced to syrupy consistency, turning often (2 to 3 minutes).

5. Serve on warmed individual plates sprinkled with parsley or dill.

YIELD: Serves 4

Per serving:
With dill

	CALORIES	SODIUM
	207	113
	No appreciable difference	

Tart and Tangy Chicken Breasts (10 minutes)

A new combination of herbs and spices, and a new use for concentrated grapefruit juice, creates a chicken dish with an intriguing new flavor.

Use iron skillet

1½ pounds boned and skinned chicken breasts, ¼ inch thick
1 teaspoon each dried sage leaves and aniseed, crushed together
½ teaspoon each ground ginger and chili con carne seasoning (no salt or pepper added), combined
1 tablespoon peanut oil
2 tablespoons each minced shallot and sweet green pepper

1 teaspoon minced garlic
2 tablespoons frozen grapefruit juice concentrate (no sugar added)
2 teaspoons tomato paste (no salt added)
¼ cup Delicious Chicken Stock (page 162)

1. Wash chicken and dry thoroughly with paper toweling. Sprinkle and rub with sage, anise, and spices.

2. Heat oil in well-seasoned iron skillet until hot. Spread shallots, green pepper, and garlic across skillet. Sauté for 30 seconds. Lay chicken atop mixture and sauté over medium-high heat on each side for 2 minutes, browning lightly.

3. Combine grapefruit concentrate, tomato paste, and stock in cup. Beat with fork to blend. Pour around chicken. Bring to simmering point. Spoon chicken with sauce. Cover and simmer for 15 minutes, turning and stirring once midway.

4. Transfer chicken to warmed serving platter. Turn up heat under skillet. Cook and stir for 1 minute. Spoon sauce over chicken, and serve very hot.

YIELD: Serves 4

Per serving:

	CALORIES	SODIUM
	243	120.5

Marsala Chicken (10 minutes)

Marsala is a sweet wine from Sicily with the time-honored power of transmuting veal into a dish fit for a Godfather's table. So here's an offer you can't refuse: Try Marsala on chicken instead of veal. Garlic- and shallot-scented breasts, tinted a toasty brown, and mellowed with Italian olive oil make a dish as sumptuous as ever emerged from a Sicilian *cucina*. You'll enjoy this offbeat touch, too: a tease of Indian spices.

Use nonstick skillet

½ ounce dried dark imported mushrooms, washed and broken into small pieces
⅓ cup water
1½ pounds boned and skinned chicken breasts, ¼ inch thick
2 teaspoons Indian Spice Mix (page 178), or ½ teaspoon each ground

cumin and coriander, and 1 teaspoon dried savory leaves, crushed
2 teaspoons Italian olive oil
3 tablespoons minced shallots
2 teaspoons minced garlic
⅓ cup apple juice (no sugar added)
¼ cup sweet Marsala wine

1. Place mushroom pieces in a cup with water. Let stand.

2. Wash chicken breasts. Dry thoroughly with paper toweling. Lay flat on a sheet of waxed paper. Sprinkle and rub on both sides with Indian Spice Mix or alternate seasonings.

3. Spread and heat oil in large nonstick skillet until hot. Sauté shallots and garlic for 30 seconds. Spread mixture across skillet. Lay spiced chicken breasts atop mixture, adding any spice mixture residue from waxed paper. Brown lightly on both sides over medium-high heat (about 3 minutes).

4. Pour apple juice and Marsala around sides of skillet. Heat to simmering point. Drain mushrooms, squeezing out liquid. Add to skillet. Spoon chicken with hot sauce, turning once or twice to coat. Reduce heat to simmering. Cover, and simmer for 20 minutes, turning and spooning with sauce twice at equal intervals.

5. Uncover. Turn heat up under skillet. Cook for 30 seconds. Serve chicken immediately on warmed serving platter, spooned with deep brown sauce.

YIELD: Serves 4

VARIATION: Change measurements of liquid ingredients to ¼ cup apple juice and 3 tablespoons Marsala wine; add ¼ cup Delicious Chicken Stock (page 162). At beginning of step 5, transfer chicken to warmed serving platter. Turn up heat under skillet and reduce sauce by half. Spoon thickened sauce over chicken.

	CALORIES	SODIUM
Per serving:	254.5	118.5
With cumin, coriander, and savory	No appreciable difference	
Variation	253	138.5

Magic-Tasting Chicken Breasts (10 minutes)

You can't *taste* magic? Really! Prepare this simple poaching stock, add unadorned chicken breasts, just cover and simmer, serve, and—that wonderful taste *must* be magic!

Use heavy-bottomed saucepan or kettle

2   tablespoons tarragon vinegar
¼   cup each apple juice (no sugar added) and Madeira wine (Malmsey)
1   medium onion, coarsely chopped
2   teaspoons minced garlic
½   teaspoon each dried savory leaves, crushed, and ground ginger

1   tablespoon minced parsley
½   teaspoon grated lemon rind
1½ pounds boned and skinned chicken breasts, ¼ inch thick
1   jarred pimento (no salt added), well drained, cut into ½-inch slivers

1. Combine all ingredients except chicken and pimento in heavy-bottomed saucepan or kettle. Bring to boil. Reduce heat to simmering. Cover and simmer for 5 minutes.

2. Wash and dry chicken thoroughly with paper toweling. Add to sauce, turning to coat. Bring sauce to simmering point again, spooning mixture over chicken. Cover and simmer for 15 minutes, turning and spooning with sauce twice.

3. Remove from heat. Spoon with sauce and let stand for 5 minutes. Transfer to warmed serving plate. Strain sauce, pressing out juices. Pour over chicken. Garnish with pimento slivers and serve.

YIELD: Serves 4

	CALORIES	SODIUM
Per serving:	220.5	117

Incredibly Simple Aromatic Chicken
(10 minutes)

"Incredibly simple" refers to the preparation—certainly not to the taste. These beautiful butternut-brown breasts exude a delightful complex of aromatic flavors, the result of a simple triumph of technique: rapid, controlled cooking time in an iron skillet. A superb surprise!

Use iron skillet

1½ pounds boned and skinned chicken breasts, cut into 4 pieces
1½ teaspoons Barbeque Spice Mix (page 178)
3 teaspoons sweet unsalted margarine-butter blend (page 182)
2 teaspoons minced garlic
2 tablespoons each minced celery and shallots

¼ cup each dry red wine and Delicious Chicken Stock (page 162)
1 tablespoon frozen apple juice concentrate (no sugar added)
1 teaspoon grated orange rind (preferably from navel orange)
2 large sprigs parsley

1. Wash chicken and dry thoroughly with paper toweling. Sprinkle and rub on both sides with spice mix.
2. Heat 2 teaspoons margarine-butter blend in well-seasoned iron skillet until hot, spreading blend across skillet with spatula. Sauté garlic, celery, and shallots for 1 minute. Lay spiced chicken on mixture. Lightly brown on both sides (about 4 minutes), adding remaining teaspoon of blend when turning.
3. Combine wine, stock, and apple juice concentrate. Pour around chicken. Bring to simmering point, turning chicken and spooning with mixture until well moistened. Sprinkle with orange rind. Push parsley sprigs into liquid. Cover and simmer for 15 minutes, turning and spooning with sauce once midway.
4. Transfer chicken to hot serving plate. Cover to keep warm. Squeeze out juices from parsley sprigs. Turn up heat under skillet and reduce sauce to ¼ cup. Spoon over chicken and serve immediately.

YIELD: Serves 4

	CALORIES	SODIUM
Per serving:	240	124

Golden Chicken Legs (10 minutes)

Shirley Glasner, whose exquisite colorful paintings adorn my walls, is also an artist in the kitchen. Her no-nonsense cooking philosophy—"Anything that can be prepared with the fewest ingredients and with the least attendance by me. gets my vote"—is a launching pad for soaring culinary feats. These citrus-touched, pepper-flecked baked chicken legs illustrate her enchanting brisk style, as do the Delicate Shrimp Hors d'Oeuvres (page 168).

Use nonstick baking pan

Preheat oven to 400°F

4   small chicken legs with thighs (about 2½ pounds), skinned
2   teaspoons corn oil
2   teaspoons onion powder
4   dashes ground black or red (cayenne) pepper

¼ cup frozen orange juice concentrate (no sugar added)
2   tablespoons plus 2 teaspoons dry vermouth
¼ teaspoon paprika

1. Wash chicken and dry thoroughly with paper toweling. Rub all over with 1 teaspoon oil. Sprinkle evenly with onion powder and ground pepper.

2. Place in nonstick shallow baking pan. Bake in preheated oven, uncovered, for 20 minutes.

3. Meanwhile, combine and have ready orange juice concentrate, vermouth, remaining teaspoon of oil, and paprika. After chicken has baked for 20 minutes, dribble with half of orange mixture, turning and basting with pan juices. Return to oven and bake for 15 minutes. Dribble with balance of orange mixture, turning and basting again with pan juices. Bake for 15 minutes. Total cooking time will be 50 minutes. Finished chicken will be golden brown. Serve at once.

YIELD: Serves 4

	CALORIES	SODIUM
Per serving:	282	117

Mahogany Brown Chicken with Turnips
(10 minutes)

I had a letter from a woman who wrote irately, "I didn't buy a gourmet cookbook to be told to cook with *turnips*. That's bourgeois food." To which I rebutted, "Dear Madam: Any food can be *made into* a gourmet food. That's a basic principle of my cooking style." Here, I put that principle into practice to create a turnip-enhanced chicken dish delectable enough for any gourmet's table.

Use iron skillet

4	small chicken legs with thighs (about 2½ pounds), skinned, legs separated from thighs
1½	teaspoons Barbeque Spice Mix (page 178)
1	tablespoon peanut oil
¼	cup minced onion

2	teaspoons minced garlic
2	teaspoons wine vinegar
¼	cup peeled and diced yellow turnip (½-inch cubes)
½	cup tomatoe juice (no salt added)
¼	cup apple juice (no sugar added)
2	large sprigs parsley

1. Wash chicken and dry thoroughly with paper toweling. Sprinkle and rub with Barbeque Spice Mix.

2. Heat oil in well-seasoned iron skillet until hot. Spread onions and garlic across skillet. Sauté for 1 minute. Lay chicken on mixture and lightly brown on each side for 2 minutes.

3. Pour vinegar around chicken. When bubbling, turn chicken, rearranging pieces in skillet so that they are well coated with vinegar mixture. Stir in turnip. Cook for 2 minutes.

4. Pour tomato juice and apple juice around chicken. Bring to simmering point, spooning liquid over chicken several times. Push parsley sprigs into liquid. Reduce heat. Cover and simmer for 15 minutes. Discard parsley sprigs.

5. Uncover. Raise heat. Cook and turn chicken pieces until liquid is reduced and syrupy and chicken is mahogany brown. Serve at once.

YIELD: Serves 4

Per serving:	CALORIES	SODIUM
	251	143

Dark-Meat Chicken Nuggets (10 minutes)

If you love chicken legs, but hate those messy bones, these boneless nuggets of dark meat raised to eminence by an extraordinary mixture of herbs, spices, and wine, is the finger-clean dish for you.

Use iron skillet

1 tablespoon sweet unsalted margarine-butter blend (page 182)
1 medium onion, coarsely chopped
2 teaspoons minced garlic
4 chicken legs and thighs (about 2½ pounds), skinned and boned, cut into 1-inch nuggets (see Note)
½ cup dry red wine
2 teaspoons tomato paste (no salt added)
½ teaspoon prepared Dijon mustard (no salt added)

½ teaspoon chili con carne seasoning (no salt or pepper added)
1 teaspoon each curry powder (no salt added) and dried tarragon leaves, crumbled
2 tablespoons minced parsley
   Juice and rind of ½ lemon
8 large Boston lettuce leaves, well washed and dried

1. Heat margarine-butter blend in well-seasoned iron skillet until melted and hot but not smoking. Spread onion and garlic across skillet. Sauté for 30 seconds. Lay chicken nuggets atop mixture in one layer. Sauté until lightly browned all over (about 4 minutes).

2. In cup, combine balance of ingredients except lettuce, beating with fork to blend. Add to skillet. Stir ingredients to combine. Bring to simmering point. Reduce heat to low. Cover and simmer for 20 minutes, stirring twice at equal intervals.

3. Remove from heat. Stir. Re-cover and let stand for 5 minutes.

4. In the meantime, drop washed lettuce leaves into a saucepan of rapidly boiling water. Blanch for 1 minute, drain. Arrange 2 leaves on 4 warmed serving plates. Spoon chicken onto leaves, and serve immediately.

YIELD: Serves 4

NOTE: If you can't induce your butcher (try a big smile) to skin and de-bone the chicken legs, then do it yourself: Pull off skin with paper toweling, cut meat from bone, then cut into 1-inch pieces with a sharp knife. Adds 5 minutes to preparation time—that's all.

SERVING SUGGESTIONS: Marvelous with Savory Green Beans with Peppers (page 97), Bright Green Peas with Orange-Hued Pimentos (page 104), or any plain steamed green vegetable.

	CALORIES	SODIUM
Per serving:	231.5	140

Double Picnic Chicken (10 minutes)

A picnic is a good time built around good eating. That's what you'll enjoy (1) when you gobble up these *cold* orange-flavored moist, tender chicken legs in the great outdoors, and (2) when you gobble up these *hot* orange-flavored etc., etc. in your own dining room. Two picnics with one kind of dish—hence, Double Picnic Chicken.

Preheat oven to 400°F

2 tablespoons frozen orange juice concentrate (no sugar added)
¼ cup dry vermouth
1 tablespoon minced dried onions
½ teaspoon ground coriander
1 tablespoon peanut oil

4 dashes ground red (cayenne) pepper
1 teaspoon dried rosemary leaves, crushed
4 small chicken legs with thighs (about 2½ pounds), skinned

1. Combine all ingredients except chicken in a cup. Beat with fork to blend. Let stand for 5 minutes.
2. Line broiling pan with heavy-duty aluminum foil. Arrange chicken in one layer in pan. Pour orange mixture over chicken. Turn chicken several times to coat. In preheated oven bake, uncovered, for 20 minutes, turn-ing once midway. Spoon with pan juices.
3. Place under hot broiler (about 6 inches from heat) and broil on each side for 7 to 8 minutes, basting before turning and taking care that chicken doesn't burn. Baste again with small amount of sauce remaining in pan. Serve hot or cold.

YIELD: Serves 4

Per serving:

	CALORIES	SODIUM
	264.5	132.5

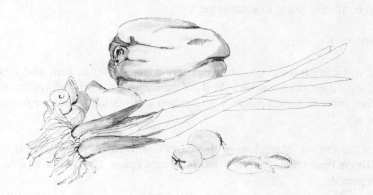

Apricot Chicken (10 minutes)

Fruity, tangy, herbaceous, sweet, colorful, stylish—for sophisticated finger-lickers.

Use nonstick skillet

4 chicken legs and thighs (about 2½ pounds), skinned and boned, legs separated from thighs
4 dashes ground red (cayenne) pepper
½ teaspoon each ground coriander, ginger, and dried savory leaves, crushed
1 tablespoon peanut oil

2 teaspoons minced garlic
1 large onion, minced
⅓ cup apple juice (no sugar added)
1 tablespoon fresh lemon juice
⅓ cup chopped dried apricots
1 whole clove
1 teaspoon honey
2 tablespoons minced parsley

1. Wash chicken and dry thoroughly with paper toweling. Sprinkle and rub with spices and savory.

2. Heat oil until hot in large nonstick skillet. Sauté chicken over medium-high heat until lightly browned. Transfer to plate.

3. Add garlic and onion to skillet (no more oil is needed). Stir and sauté until browned (about 3 minutes).

4. Add apple juice, lemon juice, apricots, and clove to skillet. Bring to simmering point. Return browned chicken to skillet, turning several times to coat. Cover and simmer for 20 minutes twice at equal intervals.

5. Stir in honey. Re-cover and cook for 10 minutes. Transfer chicken to warmed serving plate. Turn up heat under skillet. Reduce sauce for 1 minute. Spoon over chicken. Sprinkle with parsley and serve.

YIELD: Serves 4

Per serving:

	CALORIES	SODIUM
	302.5	139

Succulent Roast Cornish Hens (10 minutes)

Revelation: Cornish hens *are* chickens. Once a wild bird with a gamey flavor, they've been domesticated almost to blandness. But they're less chicken-y than the more common chicken and, in the best of the breed, taste a bit different. It's these marginal distinctions that I magnify with concoctions of diverse ingredients—ranging from yogurt to vermouth—to create birds that belong to a species all their own. Enjoy them roasted in this recipe and broiled-and-baked in the next.

Preheat oven to 375°F

1½ teaspoons Herb 'n Spice Mix (page 177)
½ teaspoon ground cinnamon
2 tablespoons each grape juice (no sugar added), fresh orange juice, and dry vermouth

1 tablespoon minced dried onions
2 Cornish hens (1½ pounds each), skinned, wing tips removed
2 tablespoons low-fat plain yogurt
¼ cup Madeira wine (Malmsey)
4 thin orange slices

1. Combine first 4 ingredients in large bowl, stirring to blend.

2. Wash and dry hens thoroughly inside and out. Add to fruit juice mixture, spooning some into cavities, and turning to coat well.

3. Place hens, breast side up, on rack in shallow broiling pan, spooning with all of fruit juice mixture. Cover loosely with aluminum foil. Position in center section of preheated oven and roast for 50 minutes, spooning with pan juices once midway.

4. Combine yogurt with Madeira. Spread over birds. Re-cover and bake for 30 minutes.

5. Split each hen in half. Serve on hot platter, garnished with orange slices.

YIELD: Serves 4

VARIATION: Fill cavities with Bulgur Stuffing with Apricots (page 109). Allow a total of 1½ hours cooking time.

	CALORIES	SODIUM
Per serving:	229	133
With Bulgur Stuffing with Apricots, add	+179	+11.5

Broiled-and-Baked Cornish Hens (10 minutes)

Preheat broiler

¼ cup grape juice (no sugar added)

2 tablespoons frozen orange juice concentrate (no sugar added)

4 whole cloves, crushed

2 teaspoons each minced garlic and minced dried onions

½ teaspoon each ground ginger and dried thyme leaves, crushed

4 large snow-white fresh mushrooms, rinsed, dried, trimmed, and coarsely chopped, or 2 tablespoons Ready Duxelles (page 180)

2 Cornish hens (1½ pounds each), skinned and split

4 thin orange slices

1. In cup, combine all ingredients except hens and orange slices and beat with fork to blend.

2. Wash and dry hens thoroughly inside and out. Place in large bowl. Pour fruit juice mixture over hens, turning several times to coat. Drain, reserving fruit juice mixture.

3. Place hens on rack in shallow broiling pan. Broil under moderate heat for 7 minutes. Spoon with some reserved mixture. Turn and broil for 7 minutes. Spoon with reserved mixture. Turn.

4. Cover pan loosely with aluminum foil. Set oven heat at 375°F and bake hens for 15 to 20 minutes, basting once midway with remaining fruit juice mixture.

5. Serve on hot platter, garnished with orange slices.

YIELD: Serves 4

SERVING SUGGESTION: Steamed Couscous in Red Wine (page 110) makes a luxurious accompaniment to this dish.

	CALORIES	SODIUM
Per serving:	259	133
With Ready Duxelles	270	135

Turkey Scallopini (10 minutes)

Your supermarket is now probably featuring a new cut of poultry dubbed "turkey cutlets." Skinless and boneless they resemble veal scallopini, are as quick and easy to prepare, and cook to the same tender deliciousness as the more expensive cut of meat. Here, they're treated with the same reverence that a scallopini receives from Milano to Ragusa—but with an amalgam of ingredients and a breading that are purely American.

Use nonstick skillet

2   tablespoons fresh orange juice
1   tablespoon evaporated skim milk
¼   cup Mixed Wheat Bread Crumbs (page 171), or crumbs made from good-quality commercial whole wheat bread
1   tablespoon unbleached flour
1   teaspoon no-fat Sap Sago cheese (page 182)

1½   teaspoons Barbeque Spice Mix (page 178)
4   turkey cutlets, cut from breast (1¼ pounds), flattened to ⅜-inch thickness
1½   teaspoons each Italian olive oil and sweet unsalted margarine-butter blend (page 182)
     Lemon wedges

1. In small bowl, combine orange juice with evaporated skim milk.

2. In cup, combine and blend bread crumbs, flour, Sap Sago cheese, and Barbeque Spice Mix.

3. Wipe cutlets dry with paper toweling. Dip into orange juice mixture. Drain. Then coat evenly with bread crumb mixture. Lay cutlets on flat plate as each piece is coated. Place in freezer for 5 minutes.

4. Heat oil and margarine-butter blend in nonstick skillet until hot. Sauté cutlets for 3 to 4 minutes on each side, or until lightly browned. Do not overcook.

5. Serve immediately on warmed individual plates, garnished with lemon wedges.

YIELD: Serves 4

VARIATION: Try same recipe with following changes: Substitute pineapple juice (no sugar added) for orange juice, and Indian Spice Mix (page 178) or Herb 'n Spice Mix (177) for Barbeque Spice Mix.

	CALORIES	SODIUM
Per serving:	253.5	128
Variation:	No appreciable difference	

Faster Recipes

Chicken with Grape Sauce (15 minutes)

The surprisingly delicate haute cuisine of the Middle Ages is my inspiration for this dish. Long before Europeans knew of sugar and lemons, the juice of grapes—"verjuice," it was called—provided sauces with sweetness and tartness. Here, mixed with herbs and spices and other familiar savories of that fabled time, grape juice is transformed into a sauce as magical as anything Merlin could have cooked up for Arthur's Round Table.

Use nonstick skillet

1½ pounds boned and skinned chicken breasts, ¼ inch thick
1 teaspoon dried savory leaves, crushed
½ teaspoon ground cinnamon
6 dashes ground red (cayenne) pepper
2 teaspoons peanut oil

1 tablespoon each minced garlic and celery
2 tablespoons minced onion
¼ cup each grape juice (no sugar added) and Delicious Chicken Stock (page 162)
1 cup seedless grapes

1. Wash chicken and dry thoroughly with paper toweling. Sprinkle and rub with savory, cinnamon, and ground red pepper.

2. Spread oil across large nonstick skillet. Heat until hot. Spread garlic, celery, and onion across skillet. Sauté for 1 minute. Lay chicken atop mixture. Brown lightly on both sides over medium-high heat (about 4 minutes).

3. Pour grape juice and stock around sides of skillet. Bring to simmering point, turning chicken several times to coat with sauce. Cover and simmer for 12 minutes, turning chicken once midway.

4. Add grapes, gently pushing them into sauce. Bring to simmering point again. Re-cover and simmer for 8 minutes.

5. Transfer chicken to warmed serving plate. Cover to keep warm. Turn up heat under skillet Reduce sauce by half. Spoon sauce and grapes over chicken and serve at once.

YIELD: Serves 4

VARIATION: Substitute ½ teaspoon ground coriander for cinnamon or ¼ teaspoon each cinnamon and coriander.

	CALORIES	SODIUM
Per serving:	226.5	120.5
With coriander	No appreciable difference	

Chicken with Almonds (15 minutes)

Among nuts, almonds rank number two in universal popularity. But after tasting them in this dish, you'll want to campaign to make them number one. (Note to discerning gourmets who are as concerned as much with the texture of food as its flavor: The chicken is textured like tender veal when it's prepared in a wok, and like delicate white meat of chicken when it's cooked quickly in a well-seasoned iron skillet.)

Use wok or iron skillet

2 boned and skinned chicken breasts (1½ pounds), washed, dried, and cut into ½-inch strips
2 teaspoons fresh lemon juice
3 tablespoons cornstarch
½ teaspoon each curry powder (no salt added), ginger, and dried savory leaves, crushed
1 tablespoon peanut oil
2 teaspoons minced garlic

1 medium sweet red pepper, seeded and julienned
¼ cup Delicious Chicken Stock (page 162)
¼ teaspoon fennel seed, crushed
2 tablespoons dry sherry
¼ cup fresh mint leaves
2 tablespoons chopped unsalted blanched almonds

1. Place chicken in bowl. Sprinkle with lemon juice, stirring to coat. Let stand for 5 to 10 minutes. Pat dry with paper toweling. Lay on a sheet of waxed paper.

2. Combine cornstarch with spices and savory, blending well. Sprinkle mixture over chicken, rubbing and turning with fingers to coat evenly.

3. Set wok on ring. Heat over high heat for 1½ minutes (see Note). Pour oil around rim. When oil drips down, add garlic and sweet red pepper. Sauté for 1 minute.

4. Lay chicken on mixture, spreading out in one layer. Sauté for 2 minutes on each side.

5. Add stock and fennel seed. Turn heat up under wok and simmer for 1 minute, turning continually.

6. Stir in sherry. Cook for 30 seconds. Transfer to warmed serving plate. Sprinkle with mint and almonds. Serve immediately.

YIELD: Serves 4

NOTE: Recipe may be successfully prepared in well-seasoned iron skillet. Measure all ingredients and place alongside skillet, just as you would when using a wok. Stir mixtures constantly, allowing a little more time for each sequence.

	CALORIES	SODIUM
Per serving:	279.5	122.5

Chicken with Leek and Tomatoes (15 minutes)

One of the great dishes of Wales is cock-a-leekie soup, the distinguishing ingredients of which are chicken and leeks. One of the memorable delights of Italian cookery is *pollo in umido*, a chicken stew enlivened with tomatoes. Here sautéed chicken is embellished with a sauce based on both leek and tomatoes to become one of the star attractions of my all-American gourmet cuisine of health.

Use iron skillet

1½ pounds boned and skinned chicken breasts, ¼ inch thick
½ teaspoon each ground ginger, coriander, and dried rosemary leaves, crushed
2 teaspoons peanut or Italian olive oil
1 leek (about ¼ pound), minced
1 tablespoon minced garlic
2 tablespoons minced sweet green pepper

3 tablespoons tarragon vinegar
½ cup dry white wine
1 8-ounce can tomatoes (no salt added), chopped
2 teaspoons sweet unsalted margarine-butter blend (page 182), or sweet unsalted corn oil margarine, cut into small pieces

1. Wash chicken and dry thoroughly with paper toweling. Sprinkle and rub with spices and rosemary.

2. Heat oil in well-seasoned iron skillet until hot. Spread leek, garlic, and green pepper across skillet. Sauté for 30 seconds. Lay chicken atop mixture and sauté over medium-high heat for 1½ minutes on each side, adjusting heat, if necessary, so that mixture doesn't brown.

3. Pour vinegar around sides of skillet. Cook for 1 minute. Then add wine and tomatoes. Spoon sauce over chicken. Bring to simmering point. Cover and cook over medium heat for 12 minutes, turning and stirring once midway. Transfer chicken to warmed serving plate.

4. Turn up heat under skillet and reduce liquid to ½ cup. Pour contents of skillet into food blender. Turn on machine and drop pieces of margarine-butter blend through top opening (or stop machine several times to add). Spoon over chicken and serve immediately.

YIELD: Serves 4

	CALORIES	SODIUM
Per serving:	252.5	117.5
With olive oil and/or margarine	No appreciable difference	

Beautiful Chicken-Veal Roll-ups (15 minutes)

A lovely light dish brightened by an herbaceous sauce sharpened with a touch of yogurt.

Preheat oven to 425°F

1 pound boned and skinned chicken breasts, ¼ inch thick, cut into 4 pieces

½ pound veal scallopini, flattened to ¼-inch thickness, cut into 4 pieces

½ teaspoon each ground cumin, curry powder (no salt or pepper added), and ginger

2 tablespoons minced shallots

1 teaspoon minced garlic

2 tablespoons minced parsley

⅓ cup warmed Delicious Chicken Stock (page 162)

2 tablespoons warmed dry vermouth

1 tablespoon arrowroot flour dissolved in 1 tablespoon water

2 tablespoons low-fat plain yogurt

1. Wipe chicken and veal pieces dry with paper toweling. Combine spices in a cup. Sprinkle and rub half of mixture over chicken. Lay veal slices atop chicken slices. Sprinkle with balance of combined spices.

2. Spoon equal amounts of shallots and garlic on center of each roll-up. Sprinkle with 1 tablespoon parsley. Roll up, tucking in ends. Place, seam side down, in one layer in 1¾-quart heatproof casserole. Pour warmed stock and vermouth around roll-ups.

Bring sauce to simmering point on top of stove. Spoon over roll-ups. Cover and bake in preheated oven for 20 minutes. Transfer roll-ups to warmed serving plate. Cover to keep warm.

3. Place casserole over heat on top of stove and reduce sauce by a half. (There should be about ⅓ cup liquid.) Whisk in arrowroot flour mixture until sauce is lightly thickened. Bring to simmering point. Whisk in yogurt. Spoon over roll-ups. Sprinkle with remaining parsley and serve at once.

YIELD: Serves 4

Per serving:

CALORIES
221

SODIUM
125

Sautéed Chicken with Yams (15 minutes)

Just toss a green salad or steam a green vegetable, serve with this rich-tasting dish—and you have *a whole meal* in record time.

Use iron skillet

2   small chicken legs and thighs (about 1¼ pounds), boned and skinned, legs separated from thighs
¾ pound boned and skinned chicken breasts
2   teaspoons Indian Spice Mix (page 178)
3   teaspoons Italian olive oil
⅓ cup coarsely chopped sweet green pepper

1   tablespoon minced garlic
1   cup (about ¾ pound) cored, seeded, and coarsely chopped fresh tomatoes
½ cup each Delicious Chicken Stock (page 162) and dry red wine
1   teaspoon tomato paste (no salt added)
¾ pound yams, peeled and cut into ⅜-inch slices

1. Wash chicken and dry thoroughly with paper toweling. Sprinkle and rub with spice mix.

2. Spread 1½ teaspoons oil across well-seasoned iron skillet. Heat until hot. Add green pepper and garlic. Sauté for 30 seconds. Spread across skillet. Lay chicken pieces on mixture and brown on both sides (about 6 minutes), adding balance of oil (1½ teaspoons) when turning.

3. Add tomatoes. Cook for 1 minute.

4. Combine stock, wine, and tomato paste. Pour around chicken. Bring to simmering point. Spoon hot mixture over chicken. Cover and simmer for 12 minutes, turning and spooning with sauce once midway.

5. Add yams, taking care that they're immersed in liquid. Bring to simmering point. Re-cover and cook for 8 minutes. Transfer chicken to center of hot serving platter. Surround with yams. Turn up heat under skillet and reduce sauce to ⅓ cup. Spoon over chicken and yams, and serve immediately.

YIELD: Serves 4 or 5

	CALORIES	SODIUM
Per serving, serves 4:	326	153.5
Per serving, serves 5:	260.5	122.5

Baked Ginger Chicken (15 minutes)

Ginger, that impishly hot and pungent spice, is here mellowed by a balanced blend of sweet herbs to give you a savory specialty as delectable as it is daring.

Use iron skillet

Preheat oven to 400°F

4	small chicken legs with thighs (about 2½ pounds), skinned, legs separated from thighs	1	large sprig parsley
1	tablespoon ground ginger	1	cup canned tomatoes (no salt added), chopped
1	tablespoon Italian olive oil	¼	cup dry red wine
3	tablespoons minced shallots	½	teaspoon fine herbs
2	teaspoons minced garlic	1	tablespoon fresh lemon juice

1. Wash chicken and dry thoroughly with paper toweling. Sprinkle and rub well with ginger.

2. Heat oil in well-seasoned iron skillet until hot. Lightly brown chicken on all sides (about 4 minutes).

3. While chicken is browning, in heavy-bottomed saucepan combine balance of ingredients except lemon juice. Bring to simmering point. Simmer just a few minutes or until chicken is finished browning. Spoon mixture evenly over chicken. Cover skillet tightly. Place in center section of preheated oven and bake for 25 minutes, turning once midway.

4. Discard parsley. Transfer chicken to warmed platter. Cover to keep warm. Place skillet over high heat. Stir in lemon juice. Slow-boil for 2 minutes. Sauce will be reduced and naturally thickened. Spoon over chicken and serve at once.

YIELD: Serves 4

VARIATION: Substitute equal quantity of Delicious Chicken Stock (page 162) for red wine.

	CALORIES	SODIUM
Per serving:	191.5	101.5
With Delicious Chicken Stock	190.5	107

Chicken in Madeira Sauce (15 minutes)

Shakespeare's Sir John Falstaff, that incomparable lover of good food, offered his soul for a tumbler of Madeira and a chicken leg. Taste these chicken legs (and the rest of the bird) enriched with a lusty Madeira sauce, and you'll agree with Sir John that the price was right. (Of the several kinds of Madeira wines, I prefer the exotically sweet golden-hued Malmsey. It makes a sauce as decorative as it is delectable.)

Use pressure cooker

1   3-pound broiling chicken, skinned, wing tips removed, quartered
¼   cup apple juice (no sugar added)
3   tablespoons apple cider vinegar
½   teaspoon each paprika, ground cumin, onion powder, and dried savory leaves, crushed

1   tablespoon Italian olive oil
1   tablespoon minced garlic
¼   cup Madeira wine (Malmsey)
⅓   cup raisins
½   cup room-temperature low-fat plain yogurt

1. Wash chicken. Dry thoroughly with paper toweling. Place in bowl.

2. Combine and blend apple juice, cider vinegar, spices, onion powder, and savory. Pour over chicken, turning to coat. Let stand for at least 5 minutes. Then drain (reserving marinade). Pat with paper toweling.

3. Heat oil in pressure cooker until hot but not smoking. Spread garlic across pot. Lay chicken atop garlic and brown lightly on each side (chicken will brown rapidly), turning from one side to another several times to prevent sticking. Transfer chicken to bowl. Discard garlic. Place rack in pressure cooker.

4. Combine reserved marinade with Madeira and raisins. Pour over chicken, turning to coat. Lay chicken on rack. Pour marinade-Madeira mixture over chicken. Close cover securely. Place regulator on vent pipe, and with pressure regulator rocking slowly, cook for 10 minutes. Let pressure drop of its own accord. Uncover. Transfer chicken to warmed serving bowl. Cover.

5. Reduce sauce over medium-high heat by half. Stir in yogurt. Reheat until just under simmering point. Pour over chicken and serve immediately.

YIELD: Serves 4

Per serving:

	CALORIES	SODIUM
	301	152

Roast Coffee Chicken (15 minutes)

The Mexicans, as every food lover knows, create an admirable chicken with chocolate, but no one ever before has flavored this bird with coffee. Here's a dish to excite even the most blasé gourmet.

Preheat oven to 375°F

1 3-pound broiling chicken, skinned, wing tips removed
2 teaspoons decaffeinated coffee
1 tablespoon Barbeque Spice Mix (page 178)
3 tablespoons wine vinegar

½ cup apple juice (no sugar added)
1 tablespoon minced dried onions
2 teaspoon coarsely grated orange rind (preferably from navel orange)
   minced fresh parsley

1. Wash chicken inside and out under cold running water. Dry thoroughly with paper toweling. Place in large bowl.

2. Combine balance of ingredients except parsley in heavy-bottomed stainless steel pot. Bring to boil. Reduce heat to simmering. Cook, uncovered, for 2 minutes. Remove from heat. Let stand for 2 to 3 minutes to cool.

3. Spoon some of mixture into cavity of chicken. Pour balance over chicken, turning to coat. Then stand chicken upright and drain, reserving marinade.

4. Place on rack in shallow roasting pan. Cover loosely with aluminum foil. Roast in preheated oven for 20 minutes. Spoon with half of reserved marinade. Re-cover and roast for 25 minutes. Pour balance of marinade over chicken. Baste with pan juices. Re-cover and return to oven for 10 minutes. Baste with pan juices. Roast, uncovered, for 5 minutes. (Total cooking time 1 hour.)

5. Cut chicken into serving pieces. Arrange on warmed platter. Spoon with pan juices. Sprinkle with parsley, and serve.

YIELD: Serves 4

NOTES:

1. Chicken may be cut into serving pieces, placed on rack, and roasted in 45 minutes. Follow directions for whole chicken, turning and basting twice at 15-minute intervals. Then roast for 10 minutes. Baste. Place under broiler for 5 minutes, and serve.

2. This recipe contains basic instructions for roasting a tender succulent bird with *any* of my marinades (pages 158 to 160). Just eliminate step 2.

	CALORIES	SODIUM
Per serving:	221	132

Chicken à la King (15 minutes)

Familiar, and yet *so* different.

Use nonstick skillet

1   tablespoon Italian olive oil
¼   pound snow-white fresh mush-
    rooms, washed, dried, trimmed,
    and thickly sliced
1   small onion, minced
2   tablespoons minced garlic
½   cup diced cooked chicken
½   teaspoon each ground ginger and
    dried tarragon leaves, crumbled

2   teaspoons tomato paste (no salt
    added)
¾   cup Delicious Chicken Stock (page
    162)
1   tablespoon arrowroot flour dis-
    solved in 1 tablespoon water
¼   cup evaporated skim milk
2   tablespoons minced fresh parsley
    or mint, or a mixture of both

1. Heat oil in nonstick skillet until hot. Sauté mushrooms, onion, and garlic until wilted but not brown (about 3 minutes), stirring often.

2. Add chicken. Sauté for 1 minute. Sprinkle with ginger and tarragon, stirring to blend. Cook for 30 seconds.

3. Combine stock and tomato paste in a cup. Add to skillet. Bring to simmering point and simmer for 2 minutes.

4. Slowly dribble in dissolved arrowroot flour. Mixture will thicken rapidly. Remove skillet from heat. Blend in evaporated skim milk. Return skillet to low heat and cook to just under simmering point.

5. Serve on very warm individual serving plates, sprinkled with parsley or mint.

YIELD: Serves 3

VARIATION: Substitute 1 teaspoon of any of my spice mixes (pages 177—178) for ginger and tarragon.

	CALORIES	SODIUM
Per serving:	114.5	55.5
With mint or spice mixes	No appreciable difference	

Tenderest-Ever Turkey Legs (15 minutes)

Just what the title says. Special taste treat: That exquisite mushroom sauce.

Use pressure cooker

2   turkey legs (2½ pounds), skinned
1½ teaspoons Barbeque Spice Mix
     (page 178)
1   tablespoon extra virgin olive oil
     (see Note, page 36)
¼   cup minced shallots
¼   pound snow-white fresh mush-
     rooms, washed, dried, trimmed,
     and cut into ¼-inch slices

⅓   cup each dry red wine and De-
     licious Chicken Stock (page 162)
1   teaspoon prepared Dijon mustard
     (no salt added)
2   parsley sprigs
2   teaspoons stone-ground yellow
     cornmeal mixed with 1 table-
     spoon water
2   tablespoons minced parsley

1. Wash turkey and dry thoroughly with paper toweling. Sprinkle and rub all over with Barbeque Spice Mix.

2. Heat oil in pressure cooker until hot. Sauté shallots over medium-high heat for 1 minute. Lay turkey on shallots. Sauté for 4 minutes, turning every minute. Add mushrooms. Stir and sauté for 2 minutes.

3. Combine wine, stock, and mustard in a cup, blending well. Add to pressure cooker. Bring to simmering point, turning turkey often to coat. Add parsley sprigs, pushing them into liquid. Close cover securely. Place regu-

lator on vent pipe and cook for 30 minutes with pressure regulator rocking slowly. Let pressure drop of its own accord. Remove cover. Transfer turkey to carving board. Cover loosely with waxed paper and let cool for 10 minutes. Then slice using very sharp knife. (An electric knife does a fine job here.) Transfer to warmed plates.

4. Place pressure cooker, uncovered, over medium heat. Stir in cornmeal mixture to thicken sauce. Cook, while stirring, for 3 minutes. Spoon sauce over turkey. Sprinkle with parsley and serve.

YIELD: Serves 4

Per serving:

	CALORIES	SODIUM
	285.5	164

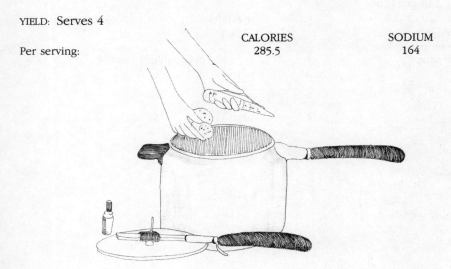

Fast Recipes

Nancy's Chicken (20 minutes)

Nancy Weil, producer of major talk shows for WABC-Radio, New York, is one of the media's most charming executives. She's also a cook of electrifying ability. Evidence: This chicken-artichoke casserole, an innovative concoction that can easily become a habit.

Preheat Oven to 350°F

1 3-pound broiling chicken, skinned, wing tips removed, cut into eighths
2 teaspoons Herb 'n Spice Mix (page 177)
1 tablespoon grated lemon rind
1 tablespoon minced dried onions
¼ cup each Delicious Chicken Stock (page 162) and dry red wine
1 tablespoon minced garlic

⅓ cup minced parsley
1 9-ounce box frozen artichoke hearts (no salt added), blanched in boiling water for 1 minute, and halved
1 tablespoon sweet unsalted margarine-butter blend (page 182) or sweet unsalted corn oil margarine, cut into pea-size pieces

1. Wipe chicken with paper toweling. Sprinkle and rub with Herb 'n Spice Mix.
2. Combine lemon rind, dried onions, stock, and wine in saucepan. Heat to simmering point. Set aside.
3. Arrange chicken in 2-quart ovenproof casserole in two layers, sprinkling half each of garlic, parsley, artichokes, and margarine-butter blend between layers and topping casserole with balance of these ingredients. Gently pour stock mixture over casserole. Cover and bake in preheated oven for 15 minutes.
4. Baste. Raise oven heat to 425°F. Cover and return casserole to oven. Bake for 45 minutes, basting with cooking juices twice at equal intervals.

YIELD: Serves 4

NOTE: Chicken will stay hot for 30 minutes, covered, after it is removed from oven.

VARIATION: Sprinkle with ¼ cup finely grated part-skim mozzarella cheese after chicken has baked for 30 minutes.

	CALORIES	SODIUM
Per serving:	275	163.5
With mozzarella	295	201
With margarine	No appreciable difference	

Heavenly Chicken Paupiettes (20 minutes)

Stuff almost petal-thin chicken breasts with a felicitous mixture of buckwheat groats and delicately seasoned eggplant sautéed with shallots and mushrooms, then mantle with a wine-based sauce stung with a suggestion of orange rind, and you create a dish of contrasting flavors and textures that's pure heaven.

Use nonstick skillet

Preheat oven to 425°F

¼ cup raw buckwheat groats (kasha)
1 tablespoon peanut oil or Italian olive oil
⅔ cup peeled and diced eggplant
2 tablespoons minced shallots
2 large fresh mushrooms, rinsed, dried, trimmed, and coarsely chopped
1½ teaspoons Herb 'n Spice Mix (page 177)

1½ pounds boned and skinned chicken breasts, ¼ inch thick, cut into 4 pieces
¼ cup each Delicious Chicken Stock (page 162) and dry white wine
1 teaspoon grated orange rind (preferably from navel orange)
1 tablespoon arrowroot flour

1. Drop kasha into half-filled saucepan of boiling water. Boil for exactly 5 minutes. Drain. Transfer to bowl.

2. Heat oil in nonstick skillet until hot. Sauté eggplant, shallots, and mushrooms until lightly browned, sprinkling with ¾ teaspoon Herb 'n Spice Mix, and stirring constantly (about 3 minutes). Add to bowl with kasha. Stir to combine.

3. Wipe chicken pieces dry with paper toweling. Sprinkle and rub balance of Herb 'n Spice Mix on both sides of chicken pieces. Lay flat. Spoon equal amount of filling on center of each piece of chicken. Fold over sides. Place seam down in one layer in 1¾-quart ovenproof casserole.

4. Heat stock, wine, and orange rind until simmering. Pour around paupiettes, spooning them with liquid several times. Cover and bake in preheated oven for 20 minutes, basting once midway. Transfer paupiettes to warmed serving plate. Cover to keep warm.

5. Place casserole over medium heat. Reduce liquid for 1 minute. Then whisk in arrowroot flour. Whisk and cook until bubbly and lightly thickened (about 1 minue). Pour any residue of cooking liquid from serving plate into saucepan. Whisk until blended. Pour over paupiettes and serve at once.

YIELD: Serves 4

NOTE: Paupiettes may be prepared through step 3 well ahead of cooking time then refrigerated. Let stand at room temperature for 30 minutes before continuing to step 4.

VARIATION: Substitute for kasha, 1/4 cup bulgur soaked in water for 30 minutes and drained.

	CALORIES	SODIUM
Per serving:	267.5	121.5
With olive oil	No appreciable difference	
With bulgar:	282.5	121.5

Julienne Chicken with Asparagus (20 minutes)

Here, small matchlike sticks of tender rose-tinted chicken, accompanied by firm emerald-bright asparagus, and flavored elegantly with a garlic-accented sauce, provide a dish to delight the most devout gastronome. For a complete meal, serve over a bed of just-cooked spaghetti, add a sparklingly fresh green salad—and enjoy a superb dining experience.

Use wok

2   tablespoons cornstarch
2   teaspoons Barbeque Spice Mix (page 178)
1 1/4 pounds boned and skinned chicken breasts
4   teaspoons peanut oil
3   teaspoons minced garlic
1   teaspoon peeled and shredded fresh ginger (optional)
1/2 pound fresh mushrooms, washed, dried, trimmed, and cut into 1/4-inch slices

1   pound fresh asparagus, tough ends removed, cut into diagonal 1-inch slices
1/2 cup Delicious Chicken Stock (page 162)
3   tablespoons dry sherry
1   tablespoon tomato paste (no salt added)

1. In bowl, combine and blend cornstarch with Barbeque Spice Mix. Sprinkle half of mixture onto sheet of waxed paper.

2. Wash chicken and dry thoroughly with paper toweling. Cut into 1/4-inch julienne strips (see Note 1). Lay strips on spice mixture. Then sprinkle chicken with balance of spice mixture, turning to coat evenly.

3. Place wok on ring (see Note 2). Heat over high heat for 1 1/2 minutes. Pour 2 teaspoons oil around rim. When oil drips down, add 1 1/2 tea-

spoons garlic and ½ teaspoon ginger. Stir-fry for 30 seconds. Add chicken and stir-fry for 3 minutes. Transfer contents of wok to dish.

4. Pour balance of oil (2 teaspoons) around rim of wok. When oil drips down, add balance of garlic (1½ teaspoons) and remaining ½ teaspoon ginger. Stir-fry for 30 seconds. Add mushrooms and asparagus. Stir-fry for 2 minutes. Return chicken to wok, stirring to combine all ingredients.

5. In cup, combine stock, sherry, and tomato paste, beating with fork to blend. Pour around rim of wok. Cover and cook for 2 minutes. Serve immediately on warmed individual plates.

YIELD: Serves 4

NOTES:

1. Chicken breasts will julienne-slice rapidly if chicken is frozen first, partially defrosted, and then sliced. If you're a working person, take frozen chicken out of your freezer compartment and place it in the refrigerator before you leave for work in the morning; it should be just perfect for quick slicing by five o'clock.

2. Recipe may be prepared in large nonstick skillet allowing a bit more cooking time over medium heat for each step. Texture will be less crisp-tender.

VARIATION: Drop 3 ounces thin spaghetti into rapidly boiling water. Cook for 8 minutes. Drain well. Add to mixture after stock, sherry, and tomato paste have cooked for 2 minutes. Serves 5.

	CALORIES	SODIUM
Per serving:	273	120.5
With ginger	No appreciable difference	
With spaghetti, serves 5	312	96.5

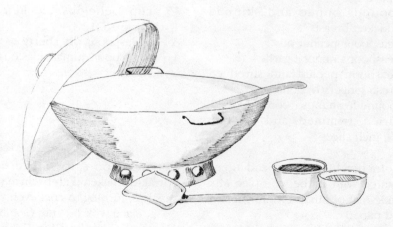

Chameleon Broiled Fish Fillets (10 minutes)

The chameleon, as who doesn't know, is a small animal with the eye-popping faculty of changing its color. This chameleonlike mixture of ingredients, as you're about to discover, is a snazzy combination with an equally astounding quality of changing its flavor. Try it on an array of different kinds of fish fillets, and experience one fresh delight after another, as the mixture transforms itself into a subtly new taste sensation time after time.

Preheat broiler

1   tablespoon sweet unsalted margarine-butter blend (page 182)
1   tablespoon Ready Duxelles (page 180) or 3 large snow-white fresh mushrooms, washed, dried, trimmed, and minced
2   tablespoons fresh lemon juice Grated rind from ½ lemon
2   tablespoons minced shallots

1½   teaspoons dried tarragon leaves, crumbled
½   teaspoon dried chervil leaves, crumbled
6   dashes ground red (cayenne) pepper
2   dashes Tabasco sauce
1½   pounds fish fillets

1. Combine all ingredients except fish in Pyrex cup set in a saucepan of hot water. Heat until margarine-butter blend is melted, and all ingredients are warm (about 3 minutes). Stir to blend.

2. Wash fillets. Dry thoroughly on paper toweling. Spoon half of warmed mixture into shallow broiling pan. Cover with fillets. Spoon balance of mixture evenly over fillets. Let stand for 5 minutes.

3. Broil 4 inches from heat for 12 minutes, spooning with sauce twice. (Cooking time will vary with thickness of fillets.) Serve immediately.

YIELD: Serves 4

VARATIONS:

1. Sprinkle 2 tablespoons finely grated part-skim mozzarella cheese over fish after it has broiled for 10 minutes. Spoon with sauce and set under broiler for 2 minutes or until cheese bubbles.

2. Substitute 2 teaspoons Herb 'n Spice Mix (page 177) for tarragon and chervil leaves.

Per serving:	CALORIES	SODIUM
With lemon sole,		
gray sole, or flounder	173	160.5
With mushrooms	173	162.5
With mozzarella	178	180
With sea bass	222	143
With mushrooms	222	145.5
With mozzarella	227	160.5
With Herb 'n Spice Mix	No appreciable difference	

Fillet of Sole with Creamy Mushroom Sauce (10 minutes)

Gray sole is my favorite, but no matter which other sole you choose—lemon, English, Dover, Torbray, megrim, or petrale (which isn't a sole at all, but a brill)—you'll find this dish one of the quickest and most satisfying you'll ever concoct. Just imagine: tender, delicate sole fillets espoused to a taste-tingling potpouri of herbs, spices, and mushrooms, then simmered gently with white wine, and finally enriched with milk, cheese, and flour to create a sauce as sleek as it is subtle—all ready for the skillet in less than 10 fast-flying minutes.

Use large nonstick skillet

1½ pounds fillet or gray sole or lemon sole

1½ teaspoons dried tarragon leaves, crumbled

½ teaspoon curry powder (no salt or pepper added)

1 teaspoon each peanut oil and sweet unsalted margarine-butter blend (page 182)

¼ cup each minced onion and shallots

½ pound snow-white fresh mushrooms, rinsed, dried, trimmed, and thinly sliced

½ cup white wine or dry vermouth

2 teaspoons unbleached flour

2 tablespoons evaporated skim milk

1 tablespoon grated part-skim mozzarella cheese

2 tablespoons minced parsley

1. Wash fish and dry well with paper toweling. In cup combine tarragon with curry powder. Sprinkle and rub over both sides of fish.

2. Heat oil and margarine-butter blend in skillet until hot. Add onion and shallots and half of mushrooms. Sauté for 2 minutes. Arrange fillets over mixture. Strew balance of mushrooms over fish. Dribble wine over mixture. Bring to simmering point, spooning liquid over mélange several times. Cover and simmer for 10 minutes, spooning with sauce once midway.

3. Uncover. Turn heat up so that liquid bubbles gently. Cook for 1 minute. Reduce heat to simmering.

4. Combine and blend flour, milk, and grated cheese, beating with fork to blend. Pour around fish, stirring and basting as sauce thickens. Cook for 2 minutes. Serve at once on warmed individual plates, sprinkled with minced parsley.

YIELD: Serves 4

	CALORIES	SODIUM
Per serving:	204	164
With vermouth	No appreciable difference	

Fillet of Flounder with Mustard Sauce

(10 minutes)

The flounder, like soles and other flatfish, is prized in my cuisine because of its low, low fat/saturated fat content, and its high, high willingness to bend to my culinary whims. In this dish, naturally bland fillets eagerly assume a sassy new character as they're clothed in a pungent sauce, brassy with the sting of mustard. A delightful transformation!

·Preheat broiler

1½ pounds fresh flound fillets, cut into 4 serving pieces
1½ teaspoons each peanut oil and sweet unsalted margarine-butter blend (page 182), plus ¼ teaspoon
1 teaspoon prepared Dijon mustard (no salt added)
1 teaspoon Herb 'n Spice Mix (page 177)

1 tablespoon fresh lemon juice
4 teaspoons dry vermouth
2 tablespoons minced scallion, including tender green part
1 tablespoon minced parsley
2 tablespoons Mixed Wheat Bread Crumbs (page 171)

1. Wash fish and dry thoroughly with paper toweling.

2. In cup, combine oil, 1½ teaspoons margarine-butter blend, mustard, and Herb 'n Spice Mix. Mash with fork to blend. Stir in lemon juice, vermouth, scallion, and parsley. Mixture will be thick.

3. Grease shallow broiling pan with remaining margarine-butter blend (¼ teaspoon).

4. Spread thin layer of mixture on one side of fillets. Lay in prepared pan, coated side down. Spread balance of mixture on fillets.

5. Broil close to heat for 6 minutes. Spoon with sauce. Sprinkle with bread crumbs. Broil until fish flakes easily when tested with fork (about 4 minutes). Serve on warmed individual plates.

YIELD: Serves 4

NOTE: Cooking time will vary slightly with thickness of fillets.

VARATIONS:

1. Substitute Barbeque Spice Mix or Indian Spice Mix (page 178) for herb mix. Better still, try it all three ways.

2. Recipe is equally delicious using lemon or gray sole.

	CALORIES	SODIUM
Per serving:	181	134.5
With variations	No appreciable difference	

Celestial Sea Bass with Rice (10 minutes)

If this title seems to you to have an Oriental ring to it, it's intended to—for sea bass is the favorite of Sino-Americans here in New York. And with what ceremonial care does the Chinese cook select just the right fish to grace her table! She peers into the creature's eyes to see that they're clear and bright, lifts the gills to satisfy herself that they're clean and red, and grudgingly nods her approval only when the scales fit tight and flat against the body. Adopt this purchasing ritual, and you'll find it guarantees a succulent fresh fish if there's one to be had. Then when you've made your selection, order it filleted, and go on to cook this American Orient-inspired dish that all the Mandarins in your family will applaud.

Use nonstick skillet or wok

¾ pound fresh sea bass fillets (see Note 1)
2 tablespoons fresh lemon juice
2 teaspoons cornstarch
1½ teaspoons Indian Spice Mix (page 178)

1 tablespoon peanut oil
1 small leek, white part only, minced
1 teaspoon minced garlic
½ lemon
⅔ cup just-cooked rice

1. Wash fish. Pat dry with paper toweling. Pull out any remaining bones with pliers. Cut into 1-inch chunks. Place in bowl. Sprinkle with lemon juice, turning to coat. Let stand for 5 minutes. Then drain and roll in paper toweling to dry. Transfer to flat plate.

2. In cup, combine cornstarch with Indian Spice Mix. Sprinkle and rub mixture over fish. (Your fingers will do the best job here.)

3. Heat oil in skillet until hot. Spread leek and garlic across skillet. Sauté for 1 minute. Lay fish in one layer atop mixture. Sauté over medium-high heat on both sides until delicately browned (6 to 7 minutes). Sprinkle with juice of lemon. Serve immediately over bed of rice.

YIELD: Serves 2

NOTES:

1. A 1¾-pound whole sea bass will yield about ¾ pound fillets.

2. Cut cooking time in half by preparing dish in wok. Here's how: Place wok on ring. Heat over high heat for 1½ minutes. Pour oil around rim of wok. When oil drips down, add leek and garlic. Stir-fry for 30 seconds (do not burn). Add fish. Stir-fry for 3 to 3½ minutes until delicately browned. Continue with balance of recipe.

	CALORIES	SODIUM
Per serving:	319.5	120

Sea Bass in Orange Sauce (10 minutes)

Loup de mer—"wolf of the sea"—is what the French call this feisty fish. And for good reason, for its appetite is as voracious as any wolf's. That quality, it seems, is transmitted to the eater. Because just after one taste of the firm white flesh, as it's cosseted here with a creamy citrus-rich sauce touched lightly with savory spices, our appetites put a *loup de mer*'s to shame. But perish the thought of eating more than you should. Thanks to the magic to my cuisine, a single portion of this dish is as satisfying as it is stimulating.

Preheat oven to 400°F

1 tablespoon frozen orange juice concentrate (no sugar added)

2 tablespoons evaporated skim milk

4 dashes ground red (cayenne) pepper

½ teaspoon each ground ginger, onion powder, and prepared Dijon mustard (no salt added)

¾ pound sea bass fillets (see Note 1 above)

2 tablespoons minced shallots

2 tablespoons minced parsley

1½ teaspoons cold sweet unsalted margarine-butter blend (page 182), cut into pea-size pieces

1. In shallow broiling pan, combine and blend first 4 listed ingredients. Wash and dry fillets, pulling out any remaining bones with pliers. Add fillets to orange juice mixture, turning to coat.

2. Sprinkle with shallots and parsley. Then dot with margarine-butter blend.

3. Bake, uncovered, for 18 minutes, basting with sauce twice. Should flake easily when tested with fork. Serve immediately.

YIELD: Serves 2; to serve 4, double recipe

	CALORIES	SODIUM
Per serving:	239	137

Broiled Halibut Steaks (10 minutes)

For fish of the year (any year) my vote goes to—the halibut. Right, not salmon, not swordfish—halibut! The glamorous cousin of the soles, this firm, snow white—fleshed fish (scorn it in your fishmongers if it's aged to gray), is enticingly flavored, and has an appealing texture that's almost meatlike. Here, the natural attributes of halibut are enhanced with a spicy sauce accented with just the right sharpness of mustard.

Preheat broiler

2 halibut steaks (1¾ pounds), cut ½-inch thick, each steak cut in half
1 tablespoon minced dried onions, or 3 tablespoons grated onion
3 tablespoons pineapple juice (no sugar added)
2 tablespoons each wine vinegar and fresh lemon juice
1½ teaspoons Barbeque Spice Mix (page 178)
1 teaspoon prepared Dijon mustard (no salt added)
1 tablespoon tomato paste (no salt added)
1 teaspoon Italian olive oil
1 tablespoon minced parsley
Lemon wedges

1. Wash fish and dry thoroughly with paper toweling.

2. Combine balance of ingredients except lemon in a cup, beating with fork to blend. (If using dried onion, let stand for 5 minutes.)

3. Place fish on rack in broiling pan. Coat with half of mixture. Broil fairly close to heat for 8 minutes. Turn. Spread with balance of mixture. Return to broiler for 8 to 10 minutes. Fish should flake easily when tested with fork.

4. Serve on hot plates garnished with lemon wedges.

YIELD: Serves 4

NOTE: Makes a marvelous luncheon treat served cold the next day.

	CALORIES	SODIUM
Per serving:	249	113
With grated onion	No appreciable difference	

Wonderful Skillet Salmon (10 minutes)

The wonderful skillet is a nonstick skillet. The wonderful salmon is our native Pacific or Atlantic salmon. And the wonderful news is a new wonderful way to prepare this wonderful fish. Wonderful!

Use nonstick skillet

¼ cup cornstarch
½ teaspoon Herb 'n spice mix (page 177)
2 tablespoons evaporated skim milk
4 fresh salmon steaks (1½ pounds)

1 tablespoon each peanut oil and sweet unsalted margarine-butter blend (page 182)
2 tablespoons minced shallots
Lemon wedges

1. In wide bowl, combine and blend cornstarch with Herb 'n Spice Mix. Pour milk into another wide bowl.

2. Wipe salmon steaks dry with paper toweling. Dip each slice into milk. Drain off excess. Then dip both sides of fish into cornstarch mixture, shaking off excess.

3. Heat oil and margarine-butter blend in nonstick skillet until hot. Spread shallots across skillet. Sauté for 1 minute. Lay salmon atop shallots.

Sauté over medium heat for 5 minutes. Turn. Sauté for 5 minutes. Cook and turn twice more at 5-minute intervals, spooning with oil mixture from time to time, and regulating heat so that shallots do not brown too rapidly. Total cooking time will be about 20 minutes, depending upon thickness of steaks. Finished fish will be browned on the outside and moist inside.

4. Serve on individual warmed plates, garnished with lemon wedges.

YIELD: Serves 4

Per serving:

	CALORIES	SODIUM
	280.5	81.5

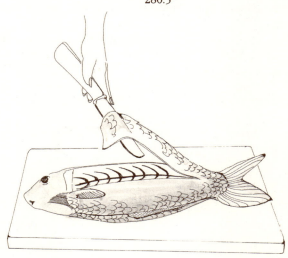

Tangy Swordfish Steaks (10 minutes)

In New England kitchens, swordfish—that most unfishy of all fish—is broiled lightly, then served with butter, parsley, and lemon wedges. That's a traditional way to serve swordfish, and it's delicious. In my New York kitchen, I delete the butter (of course), retain the parsley and lemon wedges, and add my aromatic Herb 'n Spice Mix *plus*—and no swordfish was ever treated to this imaginative touch before—orange juice. This is the new chic gourmet cuisine of health way to serve swordfish, and it's even more delicious.

Preheat broiler

3   tablespoons each wine vinegar and fresh orange juice
1½   teaspoons Herb 'n Spice Mix (page 177)
1   tablespoon minced shallots (optional)

1   tablespoon minced parsley
1½   pounds swordfish, ¾ inch thick, cut into 4 serving pieces
    Lemon wedges

1. Combine all ingredients except fish and lemon in cup, blending well.

2. Wash fish and pat dry with paper toweling. Lay on plate. Pour vinegar mixture over fish, turning to coat. Let stand for 2 minutes. Drain, reserving marinade.

3. Arrange fish on rack in shallow broiling pan. Broil 4 to 5 inches from heat for 8 minutes. Spoon with marinade and turn. Broil for 8 minutes or until done. When done, fish should flake easily when tested with fork.

4. Serve immediately on warmed individual plates, spooned with pan juices and garnished with lemon wedges.

YIELD: Serves 4

VARIATION: If your "mix" jar is depleted, substitute ¾ teaspoon each curry powder (no salt or pepper added) and dried tarragon leaves, and 8 dashes ground red (cayenne) pepper.

	CALORIES	SODIUM
Per serving:	215	90.5
Variation	No appreciable difference	

Tender Broiled Scallops (10 minutes)

This is a Coquilles St. Jacques in which the oh-so-caloric Mornay dressing is replaced with a light and engaging sauce, piquant with touches of paprika, cayenne, and ginger. (But how do I dare call my dish a Coquilles St. Jacques after I've deleted the Mornay? Because *Coquilles St. Jacques* simply means—scallops.) Of the two varieties of this saltwater mollusk, the bay scallops earn a favored place in my kitchen because they're so much more tender and delicately flavored than their deep-sea cousins.

Preheat broiler

1½ pounds bay scallops
2 tablespoons each wine vinegar, fresh lime juice, and tomato juice (no salt added)
½ teaspoon onion powder
¼ teaspoon each ground ginger and paprika

4 dashes ground red (cayenne) pepper
1 tablespoon dried minced onions
1 tablespoon minced parsley
Lemon wedges

1. Wash and dry scallops. Cut each one in half. Place in small bowl.

2. Combine balance of ingredients except lemon in a jar. Shake to blend. Let stand for 5 minutes. Shake again and pour over scallops, turning to coat. Let marinate for at least 5 minutes. Drain, reserving solids.

3. Arrange scallops in one layer in shallow broiling pan. Strew reserved solids over them. Broil under high heat for 10 to 12 minutes, turning every 3 minutes.

4. Serve on warmed individual serving plates, spooned with pan juices, and garnished with lemon wedges.

YIELD: Serves 4

NOTE: Do regard seriously the sodium statistic and be sure to include it in your calculations when you are working out your daily menu.

	CALORIES	SODIUM
Per serving:	146	438

Faster Recipes

Gray Sole Roll-ups in Red Wine (15 minutes)

"Sole," comments L. Patrick Coyle, that doyen of all things gastronomic, "is the favorite fish of those who don't eat much fish, because its flavor is not fish." To which, the equally esteemed food connoisseur, Waverly Root, adds, "Sole is one of those foods which can enter into an endless number of combinations because . . . it serves admirably to carry the tastes of other foods."

Here I've taken advantage of these two exceptional qualities of sole to create a divertingly original dish. Sparklingly fresh fillets of gray sole, wrapped around an herbaceous bread stuffing, and swathed in a daring sauce of mustard-accented red (not white) wine make a happy surprise for even the most reluctant fish eater—and the ardent fish lover as well.

Preheat oven to 425°F

4	thin fillets of gray sole (1½ pounds)	2	tablespoons minced shallots
2	teaspoons fresh lemon juice	2	tablespoons minced parsley
1½	teaspoons Herb 'n Spice Mix (page 177)	3	teaspoons sweet unsalted margarine-butter blend (page 182)
2	slices Delicate Textured Loaf (page 171) or commercial white bread of excellent quality, crusts removed	½	cup dry red wine
		¼	cup water
		½	teaspoon each prepared Dijon mustard (no salt added) and tomato paste (no salt added)

1. Wash fillets and dry thoroughly with paper toweling. Rub with lemon juice. Let stand for 5 minutes. Then pat with paper toweling to damp-dry. Lay each fillet flat. Sprinkle one side of each fillet with ¾ teaspoon Herb 'n Spice Mix. Turn and lay flat. Set aside.

2. Tear bread into small pieces. Place in small bowl. Add shallots, balance of Herb 'n Spice Mix (¾ teaspoon), and parsley. Mash 1 teaspoon margarine-butter blend until soft. Add to bowl and blend. (Your fingers will do the best job here.)

3. Spoon and spread equal amounts of mixture on each fillet. Roll up. Place, seam side down, in 1½-quart heatproof casserole.

4. Combine wine and water with mustard and tomato paste. Pour around roll-ups. Heat on top of stove until liquid bubbles gently. Remove from heat and spoon wine mixture over roll-ups. Cover and bake in center section of preheated oven for 12 minutes.

5. With slotted spoon, carefully transfer roll-ups to warmed serving platter. Cover with waxed paper to keep warm. Place casserole on top of stove and reduce liquid by half. Spoon over roll-ups and serve.

YIELD: Serves 4

VARIATION: Change liquid mixture in step 4 to ½ cup Delicious Chicken Stock (page 162) and ¼ cup dry red wine.

Per serving:	CALORIES	SODIUM
	194	117
With commercial white bread	192	158
With Delicious Chicken Stock	194	131

Crunchy Crusted Sautéed Fillets (15 minutes)

A new delight for lovers of breaded fish fillets—crunchy and aromatic on the outside, and soft, moist, delicate, tender, and stung with a suggestion of tartness within. As fast to make as most thawed-out fast-food breaded fish—and better.

Use nonstick skillet

3 tablespoons fresh lemon juice
2 teaspoons frozen orange juice concentrate (no sugar aded)
2 tablespoons tarragon vinegar
½ teaspoon onion powder
1¼ pounds fillet of lemon or gray sole, cut into 4 serving pieces
⅓ cup Mixed Wheat Bread Crumbs (page 173) or good quality whole-wheat bread crumbs made from commercial whole-wheat bread

1 tablespoon cornstarch
1½ teaspoons Herb 'n Spice Mix (page 177)
1½ teaspoon each softened sweet unsalted margarine-butter blend (page 182) and peanut oil, combined
2 tablespoons minced shallots
½ lemon
Lemon wedges

1. Prepare quick marinade by combining and blending in a cup first 4 ingredients.

2. Wash fish and dry thoroughly with paper toweling. Lay in shallow dish. Pour marinade over fish, turning to coat. Let stand for 5 to 15 minutes. Drain.

3. Combine and blend bread crumbs with cornstarch and spice mix. Spread half of mixture across sheet of waxed paper. Lay fillets atop mixture; sprinkle fish with balance of crumb-cornstarch mixture, pressing to hold.

4. Heat 1½ teaspoons combined shortenings in large nonstick skillet until hot. Sprinkle skillet with shallots. Sauté for 30 seconds over medium heat. Lay fish on shallots. Sauté until golden brown, about 3 minutes. Add balance of shortening mixture (1½ teaspoons). Sauté fish until browned (about 3 minutes, depending upon thickness of fillets). Do not overcook.

5. Squeeze juice from ½ lemon over fish. Serve on warmed individual serving plates, garnished with lemon wedges.

YIELD: Serves 4

	CALORIES	SODIUM
Per serving:	182.5	115
With gray sole:	No appreciable difference	
With commerical whole-wheat bread crumbs	182.5	187

Baked Scrod Creole (15 minutes)

Scrod, young cod, is a delicate and delicious fish when it's fresh. Let me emphasize that last word. Really fresh. Absolutely fresh. Fresh beyond a shadow of a doubt. Fresh cod fillets (or any other fillets) should look moist and tightly textured, smell as clean as an ocean breeze, and spring back firmly from indentations made by your probing figures. Here such fillets are topped and bottomed with my version of a creole sauce (I dismiss the okra, replace onions with garlic and shallots, and add an inventive mix of herbs, spices, and—yes, apple juice) then baked to rich and tender perfection.

Preheat oven to 425°F

1½ pounds fillet of scrod
Juice and grated rind of ½ lemon
1 teaspoon minced garlic
1 tablespoon tarragon vinegar
1 tablespoon Italian olive oil
2 tablespoons each minced shallots, celery, and sweet green pepper
½ pound cherry tomatoes, cored and coarsely chopped

3 tablespoons apple juice (no sugar added)
1 tablespoon minced parsley
1½ teaspoons Barbeque Spice Mix (page 178)
1 teaspoon prepared Dijon mustard (no salt added)

1. Wash fish. Dry thoroughly with paper toweling. Lay in shallow dish. Combine lemon juice, rind, garlic, and vinegar. Spoon over fish, turning to coat several times. Let stand for 10 minutes, turning once.

2. Meanwhile, heat oil in heavy-bottomed saucepan until hot. Sauté shallots, celery, and green pepper until wilted but not brown (about 3 minutes). Add tomatoes. Sauté for 1 minute. Add balance of ingredients. Bring

to simmering point. Cover and simmer for 3 minutes.

3. Arrange fish in one layer in small shallow broiling pan. Spoon half of hot sauce into pan. Lay fish atop sauce. Then spread balance of sauce across fish, covering well.

4. In a preheated oven bake, uncovered, for 15 to 20 minutes, depending upon thickness of fillet. Fish should flake easily when tested with fork.

YIELD: Serves 4

NOTES:

1. Wonderful served cold next day, garnished with lemon wedges.

2. For quickest preparation of garlic, shallots, celery, green pepper, and tomatoes, use food processor. In workbowl fitted with steel blade, combine 1 large clove garlic, halved, 2 large quartered shallots and ½ rib celery, sliced. Turn machine on/off 3 or 4 times (do not puree). Transfer to dish. Add green pepper and halved tomatoes. Process on/off 4 times.

	CALORIES	SODIUM
Per serving:	198	143.5

Baked Codfish in White Wine (15 minutes)

Because cod is so common (it was once known as "the poor man's friend") its absence on gourmet menus doesn't evoke mass protests from food cognoscenti. But it should, because fresh cod, treated with reverence in the kitchen, is one of the finest of edibles. When, for example, herbed-and-spiced codfish steaks, gently bathed in white wine, are cooked briefly and beautifully on top of the stove, then lightly crumbed, cheese-dotted, and oven-baked to perfection, you achieve a dish any gourmet would salute. Prove it to yourself with this recipe.

Use nonstick skillet and iron skillet

Preheat oven to 375°F

4 slices codfish (2 pounds with bone)

2 teaspoons Indian Spice Mix (page 178)

1½ teaspoons each Italian olive oil and sweet unsalted margarine-butter blend (page 182)

1 tablespoon minced garlic

½ cup minced onions

⅓ cup white wine or dry vermouth

1 lemon, thinly sliced

3 tablespoons each Mixed Wheat Bread Crumbs (page 171) or crumbs made from good quality enriched white bread

3 tablespoons grated part-skim mozzarella cheese

2 teaspoons sweet unsalted margarine-butter blend, cut into pea-size pieces

2 tablespoons minced parsley

1. Wash fish and wipe dry with paper toweling. Sprinkle and rub with spice mix on both sides.

2. Heat oil and margarine-butter blend in well-seasoned iron skillet until hot (do not brown). Add garlic and onions. Sauté for 1 minute. Lay fish on mixture. Sauté for 1½ minutes on each side.

3. Pour wine or vermouth around fish. Bring to simmering point. Gently spoon over fish.

4. Lay lemon slices atop fish.

5. Combine bread crumbs with

mozzarella cheese. Sprinkle over fish. Dot with margarine-butter blend; sprinkle with parsley. Bake in preheated oven, uncovered, for 18 to 20 minutes. Fish should flake easily when tested with fork. Serve immediately on warmed individual plates.

YIELD: Serves 4

VARIATION: Herb 'n Spice Mix (page 177) may be substituted for Indian Spice Mix.

SERVING SUGGESTIONS: Minted Corn and Peppers (page 101), or Bright Green Peas with Orange-Hued Pimentos (page 104) are delicious accompaniments to this dish.

	CALORIES	SODIUM
Per serving:	251	174.5
With vermouth	255.5	175
With commercial white bread crumbs	249	203.5
With Herb 'n Spice Mix	No appreciable difference	

Exquisite Shrimp with Snow Peas (15 minutes)

. . . and leeks, mushrooms, pineapple tidbits, and a constellation of other intriguing comestibles. The result is a delicate, crunchy dish that's as enticing as it is sophisticated.

Use wok or nonstick skillet

1 tablespoon cornstarch
2 teaspoons Indian Spice Mix (page 178)
1 pound shrimp, shelled and deveined
4 teaspoons peanut oil
1 tablespoon minced garlic
½ teaspoon finely grated lemon rind
2 ounces snow peas, washed, dried, stems and strings removed

1 leek, white section, sliced into ⅜-inch pieces (about ¾ cup)
¼ pound fresh mushroooms, washed, dried, trimmed, and cut into ¼-inch slices
¼ cup each Delicious Chicken Stock (page 162) and dry white wine
½ cup drained pineapple tidbits packed in pineapple juice (no sugar added)

1. In cup, combine cornstarch with Indian Spice Mix.

2. Dry shrimp well with paper toweling. Transfer to flat plate. Sprinkle and rub with cornstarch mixture, coating evenly. (Your fingers will do the best job here.)

3. Place wok on ring. Heat over high heat for 1½ minutes. Pour 2 tea-

spoons oil around rim of wok. When oil drips down, add half of minced garlic (1½ teaspoons). Stir-fry for 30 seconds. Add shrimp, spreading across wok in one layer. Stir-fry for a total of 3 minutes. (Shrimps will brown slightly.) Sprinkle with lemon rind. Transfer to plate. Do not cover.

4. Pour remaining 2 teaspoons of

oil around rim of wok. Add remaining 1½ teaspoons of garlic. Stir-fry snow peas and leek for 2 minutes. Then add mushrooms, stirring rapidly for 1 minute. Return shrimps to wok and combine.

5. Pour stock and wine around rim of wok. Add pineapple tidbits. Bring to simmering point. Simmer, uncovered, for 2 minutes. Transfer to warmed, uncovered, serving bowl. Serve immediately.

YIELD: Serves 3

NOTES:

1. Good quality shelled frozen shrimp (11 to 12 ounces) and 2 ounces frozen snow peas may be used, provided that both ingredients are defrosted and well dried before using.

2. Dish may be prepared in nonstick skillet allowing a bit more cooking time over medium heat for each step. Texture will be less crisp-tender.

	CALORIES	SODIUM
Per serving:	228	164

New-Style Fish Stew (15 minutes)

Do you know what the following dishes have in common: ukha, matelote, soliankha, waterzooi, pauchose, bourride, chiberta, bouillinade des pêcheurs, zuppa di pesce, and bouillabaisse? You're right. They're all fish stews. And what do all fish stews have in common? Longish cooking time. So how can a fish stew be included in a collection of fast, faster, fastest creations? By inventing a new style for stew making in which slow-boiling is replaced by rapid sautéing and minimal simmering. And the taste? Just as new-style as the technique: sophisticated, seductive, and satisfying.

Use nonstick skillet

1 cup canned tomatoes (no salt added), chopped

¼ cup apple juice (no sugar added)

3 tablespoons minced parsley

2 tablespoons dry sherry

1¼ pounds fillet of lemon sole

2 teaspoons Indian Spice Mix (page 178)

1 tablespoon each sweet unsalted margarine-butter blend (page 182) and Italian olive oil

¼ pound snow-white fresh mushrooms, rinsed, dried, trimmed, and sliced

1 medium onion, coarsely chopped

2 teaspoons minced garlic

1 tablespoon wine vinegar

1. Combine tomatoes, apple juice, parsley, and sherry in 1½-quart heavy-bottomed saucepan. Place over low heat.

2. Wash fish and dry with paper toweling. Sprinkle and rub both sides with spice mix. Cut into 1-inch chunks. Set aside.

3. Heat 1½ teaspoons each margarine-butter blend and oil in nonstick skillet until hot. Sauté mushrooms, onion, and garlic over medium-high heat until softened (about 4 minutes), stirring continually. Add wine vinegar. Cook for 1 minute. Transfer to saucepan with tomato mixture.

4. Heat remaining 1½ teaspoons margarine-butter blend and oil in skillet. Sauté fish for 2 minutes on each side. Pour heated tomato-onion mixture gently over fish. Cover and simmer for 7 minutes.

5. Turn into hot tureen or warmed individual soup plates, and serve.

YIELD: Serves 4

VARIATION: Substitute 1¼ pounds codfish fillets for lemon sole; a different flavor— but extraordinarily delicious.

SERVING SUGGESTION: Boiled potatoes make a perfect accompaniment to this delicious well-prepared dish.

	CALORIES	SODIUM
Per serving:	213.5	122
With codfish	No appreciable difference	

Fast Recipes

Baked Stuffed Red Snapper (20 minutes)

Bright-rose and elegant, the red snapper is as lovely to gaze upon as it is to feast on. Here the whole fish (far more moist and flavorful than its fillets) is filled with an herbaceous bread stuffing, showered with white wine and sautéed shallots, then broiled impeccably to enhance the magnificent flavor of its singularly firm white flesh. A sophisticated dish that will linger long in your memory.

Preheat oven to 425°F

1   3-pound red snapper, cleaned, head left on
3   tablespoons fresh lemon juice
½   teaspoon grated lemon rind
2½   teaspoons Herb 'n Spice Mix (page 177)
⅔   cup Delicate Textured Loaf soft bread crumbs (page 171) or soft crumbs from good quality enriched commercial white bread

2   teaspoons peanut oil
¾   cup minced shallots
3   tablespoons each nonfat liquid milk and tomato juice (no salt added)
¾   cup warmed dry white wine
2   tablespoons minced parsley
    Lemon wedges

1. Wash fish inside and out under cold running water. Dry thoroughly with paper toweling. Make several ¼-inch gashes on each side of fish. Sprinkle and rub cavity and skin with lemon juice and ¼ teaspoon lemon rind. Then rub with 2 teaspoons Herb 'n Spice Mix. Let stand while stuffing is prepared.

2. In bowl, combine balance of lemon rind (¼ teaspoon), balance of Herb 'n Spice Mix (½ teaspoon) and bread crumbs.

3. Heat oil in nonstick skillet. Briefly sauté shallots until tender (do not brown, about 2 minutes). Add a third of shallots to stuffing. (Reserve balance for next numbered step.) Stir to blend. Then slowly blend in all of nonfat milk and 1 tablespoon tomato juice. Fill cavity and head with mixture. Secure opening with skewers, or sew up.

4. Line a shallow roasting pan with heavy-duty aluminum foil, choosing a pan large enough to accommodate the full length of the fish. Sprinkle half of reserved sautéed shallots across foil. Lay fish on shallots. Then spoon balance of shallots (about ¼ cup) on fish, pushing into gashes.

5. Combine balance of tomato juice (2 tablespoons) with wine. Spoon over fish. Tear off another sheet of aluminum foil large enough to cover roasting pan. Cover and bake in center section of preheated oven for 10 minutes. Baste with pan juices. Re-cover and bake for 10 minutes. Baste again with pan juices. Return to oven, uncovered, for 5 minutes. Finished fish should flake easily when tested with fork.

6. Skin fish. Serve on warmed individual plates with a portion of stuffing on each plate, surrounded by a portion of fish. Spoon with pan juices. Sprinkle with parsley and garnish with lemon wedges.

YIELD: Serves 4

	CALORIES	SODIUM
Per serving:	292	135.5
With commercial white bread crumbs	289.5	187

Gray Sole and Shrimp Paupiettes (20 minutes)

Gray sole surpasses all other American soles, those lovely flatfish whose virtues I've extolled elsewhere in these pages (pages 66 and 74); and shrimp have long been the people's choice among the crustacea. The two bounties from the sea, cooked together in a perfect blendship, are a knockout. Delicately textured on the outside, tenderly crunchy on the inside, and bathed in a rose-hued sauce of silken smoothness, the paupiettes (fillets of gray sole wrapped around a filling of chopped shrimp and compatible comestibles) are as decorative as they are delectable.

Preheat oven to 425°F

2   fillets of gray sole (1½ pounds)
1   tablespoon fresh lemon juice
½   pound unshelled shrimp
1   cup water
1   slice lemon
2   teaspoons Herb 'n Spice Mix (page 177)

3   tablespoons minced shallots
2   tablespoons minced parsley
½   cup dry vermouth
5   tablespoons tomato puree (no salt added)
4   teaspoons arrowroot flour
¼   cup evaporated skim milk

1. Wash sole. Dry thoroughly with paper toweling. Lay each fillet flat on dish. Sprinkle and rub on both sides with lemon juice.

2. Shell shrimp, reserving shells. (Devein shrimp in next step.) Place shells in strainer and rinse under cold running water. Then drop them into saucepan with water and lemon slice. Bring to boil. Slow-boil, uncovered, for 5 minutes.

3. While shells are cooking, devein shrimp under cold running water. Pat dry with paper toweling. Coarsely chop.

4. Sprinkle and rub half of Herb 'n Spice Mix on both sides of each fillet. Lay half each of chopped shrimp, shallots, and parsley in center of each fillet, spreading out to about 4 inches. Flip one end over the other on each fillet. Secure with toothpicks.

5. Place in small casserole (1¾ quart). (It's important to use the right size casserole so that the designated amount of liquid to be added will just barely cover paupiettes.) Drain liquid from shells into saucepan. Add vermouth. Bring mixture to boil. Pour around paupiettes. Cover and bake in preheated oven for 15 minutes.

6. Carefully transfer paupiettes with slotted spoon to warmed serving plate. Cover with waxed paper to keep warm. Strain cooking juices into saucepan. Over high heat, reduce by half. Whisk in arrowroot flour. (Mixture will thicken rapidly.) Remove from heat. Stir in evaporated skim milk.

7. Cut each paupiette in half. Transfer to warmed individual plates. Spoon with pretty rose sauce, and serve immediately.

YIELD: Serves 4

VARIATION: To serve cold, arrange cooked paupiettes in bowl. Spoon with sauce. Cover tightly and chill. Arrange on platter with crisp lettuce leaves and garnish with watercress and lemon wedges. Recipe may be doubled successfully using baking dish large enough to accommodate 4 large paupiettes in one layer.

SERVING SUGGESTION: Prepare a double recipe ahead of time, chill, and serve as the star of your cold buffet.

	CALORIES	SODIUM
Per serving:	191	172.5
Variation	No appreciable difference	

Lettuce-Wrapped Fish in White Wine

(20 minutes)

This is my healthfully abbreviated version of a French classic. With candlelight, and a cool glass of Pouilly-Fuissé, this dish could enchant the man in your life to burst out in French with at least, *"Je t'adore!"*

Preheat oven to 425°F

16   large romaine lettuce leaves, well washed

1½ pounds fillet of gray sole or flounder

1½ teaspoons Herb 'n Spice Mix (page 177)
    Juice of ½ lemon

4½ teaspoons sweet unsalted margarine-butter blend (page 182)

¼   cup minced shallots

2   large fresh mushrooms, rinsed, dried, trimmed, and coarsely chopped

½   cup dry vermouth

1   tablespoon apple juice (no sugar added)

2   teaspoons arrowroot flour dissolved in 1 tablespoon water

3   tablespoons evaporated skim milk

1. Drop lettuce leaves in wide pot of rapidly boiling water. Cook for 1 minute. Pour into colander and run cold water over leaves until they're cooled. Open leaves out flat and drain on paper toweling. Cut away thickest part of tough center section of each leaf.

2. Wash fish. Dry thoroughly with paper toweling. Sprinkle and rub on both sides with spice mix. Cut into 8 fairly equal-size pieces. Place 2 pieces, sandwich style, on center of each of 4 leaves. Sprinkle with lemon juice. Cover each packet with another lettuce leaf, folding in sides to hold.

3. Grease a 2-quart ovenproof casserole with ½ teaspoon margarine-butter blend. Sprinkle with half of minced shallots and mushrooms. Arrange packets, seam sides down, on mixture in one layer (cuddle them close).

4. Heat vermouth and apple juice to simmering point. Slowly pour over fish packets. Dot with 3 teaspoons shortening. Cover and bake in center section of preheated oven for 12 minutes.

5. With slotted spoon, transfer packets to warmed serving dish. Cover to keep warm. Strain cooking juices into heavy-bottomed saucepan. Reduce over high heat to about ⅔ cup. Whisk in remaining shortening (1 teaspoon) and arrowroot mixture. Pour any residue of liquid from fish packets into saucepan. Cook over reduced heat for 1 minute until thickened. Whisk in skim milk. Bring to just under simmering point. Spoon over packets and serve immediately.

YIELD: Serves 4

Per serving:
With Flounder

	CALORIES	SODIUM
	218.5	156.5
	No appreciable difference	

Soup

Fastest Recipes

Puree of Chestnut Soup (10 minutes)

The *marrons* of France, somewhat sweeter than American chestnuts, are the foundation for this velvety sherry-laced delicacy sparked with sautéed mincings of shallots and celery. Canned *marrons*, felicitously packed in water with no sugar or salt added, are available in supermarkets.

Use food mill

1	15½-ounce can water-packed peeled whole chestnuts (no sugar added)	2	tablespoons each minced shallots and celery
1¼	cups nonfat liquid milk	1	tablespoon unbleached flour
1	teaspoon Indian Spice Mix (page 178)	2	tablespoons minced parsley
1	tablespoon sweet unsalted margarine-butter blend (page 182) or sweet unsalted corn oil margarine	4	teaspoons dry sherry
		¼	cup evaporated skim milk

1. Drain chestnuts, reserving water. Place food mill over bowl. Puree chestnuts with fine blade, adding reserved water to soften mixture while pureeing. Add nonfat milk and spice mix. Whisk to blend.

2. Heat margarine-butter blend in heavy-bottomed saucepan until melted. Add shallots and celery and sauté without browning over medium heat until softened (about 3 minutes).

3. Sprinkle flour into saucepan. Stir and cook over low heat for 1 minute.

4. While stirring, gradually add chestnut mixture until smooth and lightly thickened. Stir in parsley and sherry. Bring to simmering point.

5. Gradually add evaporated skim milk. Heat and stir until just under simmering point. Serve at once.

YIELD: Serves 5

	CALORIES	SODIUM
Per serving:	162	53
With margarine	No appreciable difference	

Puree of Spinach Soup (10 minutes)

This verdant gem, luxuriously creamy, commingles a variety of elements to produce a pottage with a myriad of flavor nuances. For that reason each spoonful should be savored in unhurried leisure either hot as-is, or chilled and sharpened with the piquancy of yogurt.

Use food blender

2   10-ounce packages washed fresh spinach, tough ends removed, or 2 10-ounce boxes defrosted frozen leaf spinach
2   cups Delicious Chicken Stock (page 162)
¼   cup each sweet Marsala wine and apple juice (no sugar added)
2   tablespoons minced dried onions

½   teaspoon each ground cinnamon and freshly grated nutmeg
1   tablespoon sweet unsalted margarine-butter blend (page 182)
1   tablespoon unbleached flour
½   cup each nonfat liquid milk and evaporated skim milk
    Low-fat plain yogurt

1. If using fresh spinach, rinse, then squeeze out water. Combine fresh or frozen spinach with stock, wine, apple juice, onions, and spices in large kettle. Bring to a boil. Reduce heat to simmering. Cover and cook for 12 minutes, stirring once midway.

2. Transfer solids to food blender and puree until smooth. Return soup to kettle. Stir in margarine-butter blend.

3. In cup, blend ¼ cup nonfat milk with flour until smooth. Whisk into hot soup. Add remaining ¼ cup nonfat milk. Heat to just under simmering point. Remove from heat.

4. Stir in evaporated skim milk. Chill. Serve each portion with a dollop of yogurt.

YIELD: Serves 6

VARIATION: This soup is also delicious served hot. When reheating, take care not to boil.

	CALORIES	SODIUM
Per serving:	92.5	138
With frozen spinach	90.5	124.5

Delicate Tomato Soup (10 minutes)

Tomatoes were once known as "love apples." They're not apples, but you can easily fall in love with them. Here, they make soups which are—well, lovable. This first soup is a dainty brew; and the second is a fuller-bodied variant enriched with the flavor of mushrooms. Both, aromatic with herbs and spices, delight the texture-buds with their silky smoothness.

Use food mill

1 tablespoon sweet unsalted margarine-butter blend (page 182)
3 tablespoons minced shallots
1 tablespoon tarragon vinegar or fresh lemon juice
2 cups Delicious Chicken Stock (page 162)
2 tablespoons tomato paste (no salt added)

¼ cup apple juice (no sugar added)
1 tablespoon Herb 'n Spice Mix (page 177)
1 cup canned tomatoes (no salt added), chopped
2 tablespoons cornstarch
¾ cup nonfat liquid milk
  Popcorn (no salt or butter added)

1. In 2-quart stainless steel saucepan or waterless cooker, heat margarine-butter blend until melted. Add shallots. Stir and cook until translucent (do not brown), about 2 minutes. Add vinegar or lemon juice. Cook for 1 minute.

2. Whisk in stock, tomato paste, apple juice, Herb 'n Spice Mix, and tomatoes. Bring to simmering point.

Reduce heat. Cover and simmer for 15 minutes. With bowl underneath, pour through fine sieve or food mill, pressing out juices. Return soup to saucepan over medium heat.

3. In cup, dissolve cornstarch in ¼ cup nonfat milk. Whisk into hot soup. Then add remaining ½ cup milk. Heat until just under simmering point, and serve.

YIELD: Serves 4

VARIATION: One-third cup minced onion and 1 small clove garlic, minced, may be substituted for shallots.

	CALORIES	SODIUM
Per serving:	103.5	81
With fresh lemon juice	No appreciable difference	
Variation	No appreciable difference	

Creamy Mushroom-Tomato Soup (10 minutes)

Use food blender

1   tablespoon peanut oil
¾   pound snow-white mushrooms, washed, dried, trimmed, and coarsely chopped
1   medium onion, coarsely chopped
1   tablespoon coarsely chopped garlic
2   teaspoons Herb 'n Spice Mix (page 177)

2   teaspoons each wine vinegar and fresh lemon juice
1½   cups Delicious Chicken Stock (page 162)
1¼   cups tomato juice (no salt added)
¼   cup just-snipped dill
5   teaspoons regular Cream of Wheat
⅓   cup evaporated skim milk

1. Heat oil in large heavy-bottomed saucepan. Add mushrooms, onion, and garlic. Sauté over medium-high heat for 3 minutes, turning often. Sprinkle with Herb 'n Spice Mix. Sauté for 2 minutes, stirring to combine.

2. Add vinegar and lemon juice. Cook for 30 seconds.

3. Stir in stock, tomato juice, and dill. Bring to simmering point.

4. Sprinkle with Cream of Wheat, stirring rapidly. Partially cover. Reduce heat to simmering. Simmer for 20 minutes, stirring twice. Let cool, uncovered, for 5 minutes.

5. Pour half of mixture at a time into food blender. Puree for 30 seconds on high setting. Pour into saucepan. Puree balance of mixture. Reheat entire pureed mixture to simmering. Remove from heat. Whisk in milk. Serve immediately.

YIELD: Serves 3 or 4

	CALORIES	SODIUM
Per serving, serves 3:	165	122
Per serving, serves 4:	124	91.5

Faster Recipes

Watercress and Potato Soup (15 minutes)

To the potato's genial blandness, add watercress's delicate pepperiness and a compatible array of tongue-tingling spicy and herbaceous flavors (including that of curry), enliven with a splash of sherry—and enjoy a first course as light as it is lovely.

Use food mill

2 teaspoons Italian olive oil
1 tablespoon minced garlic
1 small onion, minced
2 teaspoons tarragon vinegar
½ pound Idaho potatoes, peeled and diced into ¼-inch pieces
3 cups Delicious Chicken Stock (page 162)
¼ cup dry sherry

1 teaspoon each curry powder (no salt or pepper added) and dried tarragon leaves, crumbled
1 bunch watercress, tough stems removed, chopped
1 tablespoon regular Cream of Wheat
¼ cup evaporated skim milk
3 tablespoons low-fat plain yogurt

1. In heavy-bottomed 2-quart saucepan or waterless cooker, heat oil until hot but not smoking. Sauté garlic and onion over medium heat for 2 minutes, stirring constantly, taking care not to burn. Add tarragon vinegar and cook for 1 minute.

2. Stir in potatoes, stock, sherry, curry powder, and tarragon. Bring to a boil. Reduce heat to simmering. Cover and simmer for 8 minutes. Add watercress. Bring to slow-boil. Sprinkle in Cream of Wheat. Stir. Simmer, covered, for 7 minutes.

3. Puree mixture in food mill into bowl (the residue of any thick stems will remain in food mill).

4. Whisk in evaporated skim milk. Then whisk in yogurt.

5. If using within a few hours, chill. Serve at room temperature or slightly chilled.

YIELD: Serves 4

	CALORIES	SODIUM
Per serving:	119.5	113

Versatile Tangy Beet Soup (15 minutes)

Versatile, because it can be served as a first course; or, with boiled potatoes and a dollop of yogurt, as a main course. Either way, this dish is a novel departure from borscht (the traditional Slavic beet soup), highlighted by the daring use of Indian spices and apple juice. Keep your taste buds open for: that underlying sweet flavor of carrot.

Use food processor (optional)

4	large shallots, peeled and quartered	2	cups Delicious Chicken Stock (page 162)
1	medium carrot, peeled and thickly sliced	½	cup apple juice (no sugar added)
		4	cloves, crushed
2	cups canned sliced beets packed in water (no salt added)	1½	teaspoons Indian Spice Mix (page 178)
1	tablespoon peanut oil	2	sprigs parsley
2	tablespoons each fresh lemon juice and apple cider vinegar		

1. Fit food processor with steel blade. Place shallots in work bowl. Process on/off 3 times until minced. Do not overprocess. Remove from bowl.

2. Add carrot and process until minced (about 6 seconds). Remove from bowl.

3. Drain beets, reserving liquid. Place beets in work bowl and process on/off 3 to 4 times.

4. Heat oil in heavy-bottomed 2-quart saucepan until hot. Sauté minced shallots and carrots over medium heat for 3 minutes without browning, stirring constantly. Add beets and sauté for 1 minute.

5. Add lemon juice and apple cider vinegar, stirring and cooking for 1 minute.

6. Stir in reserved beet liquid, and balance of ingredients. Bring to simmering point. Cover and simmer for 15 minutes. Discard parsley sprigs. Serve hot or chilled.

YIELD: Serves 4 or 5

VARATION: Serve cold with a dollop of low-fat plain yogurt atop each serving.

SERVING SUGGESTION: Small boiled and skinned red-skinned potatoes served on the side add a delicate touch of sweetness to this tangy soup.

	CALORIES	SODIUM
Per serving, serves 4:	114.5	102
With yogurt	123.5	112
Per serving, serves 5:	91.5	81.5
With yogurt	100.5	83.5
For each potato, add	+40.5	+1

Savory Lentil Soup with Chicken (15 minutes)

The favorite legume of gastronomes in our circle, lentils here serve as a foundation for a tomato- and turnip-enriched soup almost ragout-thick with nuggets of meltingly tender chicken. Makes a satisfying one-meal dish.

Use pressure cooker

¾ pound boned and skinned chicken breasts, cut into ½-inch pieces
1 tablespoon Italian olive oil
1 tablespoon minced garlic
⅓ cup peeled and diced yellow turnip
1 medium onion, minced
½ cup lentils, soaked overnight and drained
2½ teaspoons Barbeque Spice Mix (page 178)

1 cup canned tomatoes (no salt added), chopped
2 tablespoons tomato paste (no salt added)
1 tablespoon fresh lemon juice
3 tablespoons Madeira wine (Malmsey)
3 cups water
2 large sprigs parsley

1. Wash chicken and wipe dry with paper toweling. Heat oil in pressure cooker until hot. Sear chicken briefly on both sides.

2. Add garlic, turnip, and onion. Sauté mixture for 3 minutes, stirring often. Add drained lentils.

3. Sprinkle with spice mix, stirring to distribute evenly over chicken and vegetables.

4. Combine tomatoes with tomato paste, lemon juice, and Madeira. Stir into mixture. Add water. Bring to a boil. Drop parsley sprigs into pot.

5. Cover pot securely. Place pressure regulator on vent pipe and cook for 30 minutes. Cool at once under cold running water. Discard parsley sprigs, and serve.

YIELD: Serves 6 or 8

	CALORIES	SODIUM
Per serving, serves 6:	162.5	53
Per serving, serves 8:	122	39.5

Fast Recipe

Hearty Bean and Cabbage Soup (20 minutes)

This is a lip-smacking, stomach-filling, taste-tingling meal-in-itself. Meat lovers, don't pass it by: The vegetables are enriched by hunks of tender beef.

Use food processor (optional)

Use Dutch oven

½ pound crisp green cabbage (use half of 1-pound head)
4 cloves garlic, peeled and halved
1 medium onion, peeled, cut into 1-inch chunks
1 tablespoon peanut oil
½ pound lean beef, cut into ½-inch cubes
2 teaspoons Indian Spice Mix (page 178)

2 tablespoons tarragon vinegar
1 cup apple juice (no sugar added)
3 cups water or Delicious Chicken Stock (page 162)
2 large sprigs parsley
6 whole cloves
1 cup cooked dried baby white beans (see Note)

1. Fit food processor with shredding disc. Shred cabbage (or thinly slice with sharp knife). Measure out 2 cups. Turn into bowl. Fit processor with steel blade. Process garlic and onion until chopped (do not overprocess). Combine with cabbage. Set aside.

2. In Dutch oven, heat oil until hot. Add meat and quickly sear on all sides. Sprinkle with spice mix.

3. Add cabbage mixture to Dutch oven. Sauté over high heat for 3 minutes, stirring often. Add tarragon vinegar and stir to combine. Cook for 1 minute.

4. Add balance of ingredients except beans. Bring to boil. Reduce heat to simmering. Cover tightly and cook for 30 minutes.

5. Stir in beans. Bring to simmering point. Re-cover and cook for 30 minutes. Stir. Remove from heat and let stand, covered, for 10 minutes before serving.

YIELD: Serves 6

NOTE: Beans may be prepared the day before and kept refrigerated.

VARIATION: If you prefer a thickened soup, dissolve 1 tablespoon arrowroot flour in 1 tablespoon water. Dribble into soup after beans have cooked for 30 minutes (step 5).

	CALORIES	SODIUM
Per serving:	152.5	41.5
With Delicious Chicken Stock	163.5	91.5
With arrowroot	168.5	92.5

Vegetables, Grains, and Pasta

Fastest Recipes

Asparagus and Mushrooms with a Piquant Sauce (10 minutes)

Here I've married plump, verdant asparagus tips to snow-white mushroom slices, and bedecked them with a spicy sauce to produce a honeymoon of flavors.

2   teaspoons minced dried onions
¼   cup each dry vermouth and water
1   10-ounce box frozen asparagus and tips (see Note)
½   pound snow-white fresh mushrooms, washed, trimmed, and thickly sliced

1   large sprig parsley
1   teaspoon Barbeque Spice Mix (page 178)
1   teaspoon tomato paste (no salt added)

1. Place dried onions in medium-sized stainless steel or enameled saucepan. Add vermouth and water. Stir. Then add asparagus and mushrooms in alternate layers. Bring to a boil. Cover and slow-boil for 8 minutes, stirring gently twice. (Solids will reduce in volume and liquid will cover solids after 3 minutes cooking time.)

2. Set colander over bowl. Pour mixture into colander and drain well. Discard parsley sprig. Place asparagus and mushrooms in warmed serving bowl. Return drained liquid to saucepan. Add Barbeque Spice Mix and tomato paste. Cook over medium heat for 2 minutes, stirring often. Liquid will thicken slightly and reduce by one third. Pour over vegetables, and serve.

YIELD: Serves 4

NOTE: Use ¾ pound fresh asparagus when in season. Cut and discard tough ends. Slice balance of spears into 1-inch pieces, leaving the tips intact. Cooking time will be the same as for frozen asparagus.

	CALORIES	SODIUM
Per serving:	57	16.5
With fresh asparagus	No appreciable difference	

Asparagus Vinaigrette (10 minutes)

This is a vinaigrette with less oil than the classic version, proportionately more vinegar, and with herbs and spices instead of salt and pepper. One added distinction: a new and exciting flavor.

1½ pounds fresh asparagus, washed, tough ends removed
½ cup water
2 teaspoons tarragon vinegar

1 large parsley sprig
5 tablespoons Lively and Light Salad Dressing (page 134)

1. Place asparagus in wide, heavy-bottomed saucepan. Add water, vinegar, and parsley sprig, pushing sprig into water. Bring to a boil. Reduce heat to simmering. Cover and poach for 7 to 8 minutes, spooning twice with poaching liquid.

2. With slotted spoon transfer to warmed serving plate. Stir Light and Lively Salad Dressing. Spoon 4 tablespoons evenly over asparagus. Let stand for 2 minutes before serving.

YIELD: Serves 4

NOTE: Recipe may be prepared an hour ahead and served at room temperature. Cover with waxed paper after salad dressing is added.

	CALORIES	SODIUM
Per serving:	108.5	8

Cardamom Potatoes (10 minutes)

To a yogurt-tanged mix of tantalizing herbs and spices, add cardamom, and savor an exquisite overtone of flavor that's sweet and pungent and lemon-nuanced all at once. Little wonder .that cardamom seeds are known in the Orient as "grains of paradise."

3 Idaho potatoes (1¼ pounds), peeled, cubed, cooked until tender, and drained
2 teaspoons sweet unsalted margarine-butter blend (page 182) or sweet unsalted corn oil margarine
½ teaspoon onion powder
¼ teaspooon each ground marjoram and freshly grated nutmeg

½ teaspoon ground cardamom
4 dashes ground red (cayenne) pepper
3 tablespoons low-fat plain yogurt
2 tablespoons minced parsley
1 scallion, including green part, trimmed and minced
½ teaspoon caraway seed, partially crushed

1. Mash potatoes while still warm with margarine-butter blend. Add onion powder, marjoram, nutmeg, cardamom, and ground red pepper. Blend well.

2. Stir in balance of ingredients in order in which they're listed. Reheat briefly, if necessary, over simmering water.

YIELD: Serves 4

NOTE: These creamy-textured potatoes taste best if prepared just before serving.

	CALORIES	SODIUM
Per serving:	111.5	13
With margarine	No appreciable difference	

New-Style Mashed Potatoes (10 minutes)

The yam, in the West Indies and in our South, is a staple of soul food. But here, and in the recipe that follows, this country cousin of the sweet potato is the soul of two dishes distinguished by their sophistication.

½ pound yams, peeled
¾ pound Idaho potatoes, peeled
2 tablespoons minced shallots or onions
1 tablespoon minced chives
1 teaspoon curry powder (no salt or pepper added)

½ teaspoon each mild paprika and fine herbs
1 tablespoon sweet unsalted corn oil margarine or sweet unsalted margarine-butter blend (page 182)
2 tablespoons low-fat plain yogurt

1. Cut potatoes into ½-inch cubes. Cook in rapidly boiling water in stainless steel or enameled pot. Drain well in strainer. Return to pot and mash.

2. Add balance of ingredients except yogurt and mash again. Then stir in yogurt. Reheat over simmering water and serve.

YIELD: Serves 4

VARIATION: Add ½ teaspoon prepared Dijon mustard (no salt added) in step 2.

	CALORIES	SODIUM
Per serving:	137	9
With onion-margarine-butter blend, Dijon	No appreciable difference	

Pretty Mixed Potatoes (10 minutes)

Preheat oven to 425°F

1   pound russet or Idaho potatoes, peeled, cut into ½-inch cubes
½   pound yams, peeled, cut into ½-inch cubes
2   teaspoons margarine-butter blend (page 182), plus ½ teaspoon for baking dishes
2   tablespoons chopped onion or shallots

2   teaspoons Herb 'n Spice Mix (page 177)
1   tablespoon grated orange rind (preferably from navel orange)
2   tablespoons low-fat plain yogurt
2   tablespoons minced dill

1. Cook potatoes in heavy-bottomed saucepan in water to cover for 10 to 12 minutes. Potatoes should be tender but remain firm. Drain well.

2. Heat margarine-butter blend in saucepan until melted. Add onion or shallots and sauté for 1½ minutes without browning. Remove from heat. Add potatoes and mash.

3. Sprinkle with Herb 'n Spice Mix and orange rind. Stir to blend. Then stir in yogurt and dill.

4. Pile into 4 lightly greased ovenproof crocks. Bake in preheated oven for 15 to 20 minutes. Tops should be lightly browned and mixture will puff up. Serve immediately.

YIELD: Serves 4

	CALORIES	SODIUM
Per serving:	147	15.5
With shallots	No appreciable difference	

Marsala Spinach (10 minutes)

Herbed, creamed, and sweetened with Marsala, this is spinach at its elegant best without a trace of its usual bitter aftertaste.

1   10-ounce box frozen chopped spinach
½   cup water
1   teaspoon minced dried onions
1   teaspoon Herb 'n Spice Mix (page 177)

2   teaspoons sweet unsalted margarine-butter blend
2   tablespoons sweet Marsala wine
2   teaspoons arrowroot flour
¼   cup nonfat liquid milk

1. Place spinach, water, onions, and Herb 'n Spice Mix in heavy-bottomed saucepan. Bring to a quick boil, breaking up spinach with fork as it thaws (about 2 minutes).

2. Add margarine-butter blend and Marsala. Quickly stir to blend. Reduce heat to simmering. Cover and simmer for 2 minutes.

3. In cup, dissolve arrowroot flour in milk. Slowly dribble into spinach while stirring. Mixture will thicken slightly. Bring to just under simmering point, and serve.

YIELD: Serves 3 or 4

	CALORIES	SODIUM
Per serving, serves 3:	66	57.5
Per serving, serves 4:	49.5	43

Green Beans with Mushrooms and Red Wine (10 minutes)

This is the kind of dish that evokes a passionate craving for seconds. So I've helpfully limited the calorie and sodium counts to bare minimums to permit you to satisfy your craving without a tinge of guilt.

1   9-ounce box frozen French-cut green beans
⅓   cup dry red wine
1   teaspoon minced dried onions
1   teaspoon Barbeque Spice Mix (page 178)

¼   pound snow-white fresh mushrooms, rinsed, trimmed, and coarsely chopped
2   teaspoons sweet unsalted margarine-butter blend or sweet unsalted corn oil margarine
½   teaspoon no-fat Sap Sago cheese (page 182)

1. Place box of frozen green beans under hot running water for 1 minute to partially defrost.

2. Bring wine, dried onions, and spice mix to a boil in heavy-bottomed saucepan. Add green beans. Bring mixture to a boil again.

3. Add mushrooms. Cover and simmer for 5 minutes, stirring once or twice, or until mixture is totally defrosted. Drain off liquid.

4. Add margarine-butter blend or margarine. Sprinkle with Sap Sago cheese. Cover for 30 seconds. Gently stir, and serve at once.

YIELD: Serves 4

	CALORIES	SODIUM
Per serving:	68	12.5
With margarine	No appreciable difference	

Savory Green Beans with Peppers (10 minutes)

The vivid red of the peppers and the bright green of the beans make this dish as delightful to your sense of color as it is to your sense of taste. Special attraction: that herbed-and-spiced tomato-yogurt mix.

Use nonstick skillet

¾ pound fresh green beans, trimmed, cut into ½-inch slices
2 sprigs parsley
2 teaspoons peanut or Italian olive oil
1 large sweet red pepper, cored, seeded, and julienned

2 tablespoons minced shallots
1½ teaspoons Herb 'n Spice Mix (page 177)
2 tablespoons each tomato juice (no salt added) and low-fat plain yogurt, room temperature

1. Drop green beans in pot of rapidly boiling water. Add parsley. Partially cover and rapidly boil until crisp-tender (about 5 minutes). Drain. Discard parsley.

2. Heat oil in nonstick skillet until hot. Sauté sweet red pepper and shallots until wilted, stirring constantly.

Add green beans. Sprinkle with herb mix and stir to combine. Sauté until mixture is heated through. Remove from heat.

3. Combine tomato juice with yogurt. Stir into vegetables. Serve immediately.

YIELD: Serves 4

	CALORIES	SODIUM
Per serving:	63.5	17
With Italian olive oil	No appreciable difference	

Sweet and Spicy Carrots (10 minutes)

To the carrot's natural sweetness (this fleshy root was once called "underground honey"), I've added a singular mix of the tart and the pungent to create a memorable dish of contrasting flavors.

Use nonstick skillet

¾ pound fresh carrots, sliced into ¾-inch pieces
½ cup apple juice (no sugar added)
1 tablespoon sweet unsalted margarine-butter blend (page 182) or sweet unsalted corn oil margarine
2 tablespoons minced shallots

1 teaspoon Indian Spice Mix (page 178)
1 teaspoon tarragon vinegar
1 teaspoon finely grated orange rind (preferably from navel orange)
1 tablespoon minced parsley

1. Place carrots in 1½-quart saucepan. Add apple juice and enough water to cover. Bring to a rolling boil. Reduce heat to simmering. Cover and cook for exactly 9 minutes, stirring once midway. Drain.

2. Heat margarine-butter blend in nonstick skillet until hot. Add shallots and sauté for 1 minute. Add carrots and sprinkle with Indian Spice Mix. Stir gently to combine. Sauté for 1 minute. Sprinkle with vinegar and blend.

3. Sprinkle with orange rind and parsley. Stir and sauté until evenly heated. Serve immediately.

YIELD: Serves 4

	CALORIES	SODIUM
Per serving:	75	7
With margarine	No appreciable difference	

Broccoli-Leek Puree (10 minutes)

When pureed with a yogurt and spice-accented chicken stock, broccoli and leek shed their assertive flavors (cabbage-y and onion-y respectively), and blend into a subtle-flavored concoction that seems to have been made from vegetables you've never tasted before.

Use food processor

1 bunch broccoli (1½ pounds)
2 leeks, tough ends removed, well washed and cut into ½-inch slices
1 cup Delicious Chicken Stock (page 162)
¼ cup sweet Madeira wine (Malmsey)

½ teaspoon each freshly grated nutmeg and ground thyme
1 teaspoon curry powder (no salt or pepper added)
Flowerets from 4 sprigs parsley
5 tablespoons low-fat plain yogurt

1. Cut broccoli flowerets down to include 2 inches of stems. Peel back stems. (Peeling removes unpleasant bitterness and reduces cooking time.)

2. Place peeled broccoli and balance of ingredients, except yogurt, in large heavy-bottomed saucepan or waterless cooker. Bring to a boil. Reduce heat to simmering, cover, and simmer for exactly 8 minutes, pushing solids into liquid from time to time.

3. Turn into food processor and process for 5 to 6 seconds. Do not overprocess. Return mixture to saucepan. Stir in yogurt. Reheat to just under simmering point, and serve.

YIELD: Serves 4

NOTES:

1. Food blender may be used instead of processor in step 3. Blend half of cooked mixture at a time.

2. Recipe may be halved successfully.

	CALORIES	SODIUM
Per serving:	96.5	71

Sautéed Zucchini with Mushrooms (10 minutes)

The distinctive and delicate flavors of these stylish edibles are brightened by a flavorsome sauce. Secret of success: the light touch of Indian spices.

Use nonstick skillet

1 tablespoon peanut oil or Italian olive oil

2 tablespoons minced shallots

2 medium zucchini (¾ pound), trimmed, scrubbed, and cut into ½-inch chunks

¼ pound fresh mushrooms, washed, dried, trimmed, and sliced

1 teaspoon Indian Spice Mix (page 178)

2 teaspoons tarragon or wine vinegar

2 tablespoons Delicious Chicken Stock (page 162) or tomato juice (no salt added)

2 tablespoons minced parsley

1. Heat oil in nonstick skillet until hot. Sauté shallots for 30 seconds. Add zucchini and mushrooms. Sauté for 1 minute.

2. Sprinkle with Indian Spice Mix. Continue to sauté until zucchini and mushrooms are slightly softened (about 4 minutes over medium-high heat).

3. Add vinegar. Sauté for 30 seconds. Then add stock or tomato juice. Cook until mixture is well heated.

4. Turn into warmed serving bowl. Sprinkle with parsley, and serve very hot.

YIELD: Serves 4

VARIATION: Sprinkle cooked mixture with 2 tablespoons finely grated part-skim mozzarella cheese or 1 teaspoon no-fat Sap Sago cheese.

	CALORIES	SODIUM
Per serving:	60	12
With Italian olive oil	No appreciable difference	
With wine vinegar	No appreciable difference	
With tomato juice	No appreciable difference	
With mozzarella	70	30.5
With Sap Sago	61	16

Gentle Sweet and Sour Cabbage (10 minutes)

Sweetness is derived from onions, carrots, apple, raisins, apple juice, and Marsala. Sourness from lemon juice and tarragon vinegar. And gentleness from the *tout ensemble* of those ingredients simmering together to banish feistiness from the flavor of cabbage.

5   cups thinly sliced green cabbage (about 1 pound)
1   large onion, thinly sliced
2   large carrots, peeled and thinly sliced
½   cup each apple juice (no sugar added) and water
¼   cup Marsala wine

2   tablespoons each fresh lemon juice and tarragon vinegar
1   crisp sweet apple (such as McIntosh), peeled, cored, and coarsely chopped
¼   cup raisins
3   whole cloves

1. Combine all ingredients in deep kettle. Bring to a boil. Boil, uncovered, and stir for 1 minute. Reduce heat to simmering. Cover and cook for 30 to 40 minutes, stirring from time to time.

2. Let stand, covered, for 10 minutes. Serve.

YIELD: Serves 6

NOTES:
1. Taste when done. If too tart (I like it slightly tart), add 1 teaspoon honey, stirring well.
2. Flavor is wonderful if refrigerated and rewarmed next day.

	CALORIES	SODIUM
Per serving:	126	34.5
With honey	129.5	34.5

Minted Corn and Peppers (10 minutes)

Sweet corn and sweet red peppers are sautéed with a tart-and-spicy sauce dominated by mint to produce an exceptional combination of contrasting flavors. Trick of the trade: marjoram to heighten the mintiness.

Use nonstick skillet

2 teaspoons peanut or Italian olive oil
1 small sweet red pepper, seeded and julienned
2 tablespoons minced shallots
1 10-ounce box frozen kernel corn, cooked

½ teaspoon ground ginger
¼ teaspoon ground marjoram
1 teaspoon wine vinegar
2 tablespoons minced fresh mint

1. Heat oil in nonstick skillet until hot. Sauté sweet red pepper and shallots briefly until just wilted.

2. Add corn, stirring to combine.

3. Sprinkle with ginger and marjoram. Stir and sauté for 1 minute.

4. Add wine vinegar and cook until all ingredients are heated through.

5. Remove from heat. Add mint and toss. Serve immediately.

YIELD: Serves 4

NOTE: Fresh mint tastes best. If not available, substitute 1½ teaspoons dried crumbled mint in step 5.

	CALORIES	SODIUM
Per serving:	84	4.5
With Italian olive oil	No appreciable difference	
With dried mint	No appreciable difference	

Two-Way Okra-Dill Stew (10 minutes)

Okra, as every cook who ever made a gumbo knows, is a superb thickener for stews. In this vegetable stew, it has another function as well. Its distinctive tartness is allied with dill's pungency to add new flavor excitement to a seasoned mix of corn and tomatoes. Dramatic!

1 10-ounce box frozen cut okra
1 8-ounce can tomatoes (no salt added), chopped
⅔ cup frozen corn kernels
¼ cup apple juice (no sugar added)
1 tablespoon tarragon vinegar

2 tablespoons dry red wine
1 medium onion, coarsely chopped
1½ teaspoons Barbeque Spice Mix (page 178)
2 tablespoons coarsely chopped just-snipped dill

1. Combine all ingredients in heavy-bottomed saucepan. Bring to a boil. Reduce heat to simmering. Cover and simmer for 15 minutes, stirring from time to time and checking heat. Caution: The gelatinous component of okra tends to cause this vegetable to stick to the bottom of the pot when heat is too high.

2. Let stand for 5 minutes, covered, before serving.

YIELD: Serves 4

VARIATION: Serve mixture as salad. Chill, then stir in 2 tablespoons tarragon vinegar and 1 tablespoon Italian olive oil.

	CALORIES	SODIUM
Per serving:	67	8
Variation	99	10.5

Skillet Rice with Tomatoes (10 minutes)

This is actually a very special kind of rice-and-tomato stew: The liquid is absorbed in the rice! And, of course, the liquid is very special, too; as how could it not be with Marsala and apple juice, green pepper and chicken stock, and anise-scented tarragon among its ingredients. Serve as a side dish, or add cracklingly fresh salad for a light and satisfying meal.

Use nonstick skillet

1 tablespoon Italian olive oil
3 tablespoons each minced shallots and sweet green pepper
½ cup raw rice
¼ cup apple juice (no sugar added)
1 cup canned tomatoes (no salt added), chopped
3 tablespoons Marsala wine

1 cup Delicious Chicken Stock (page 162)
1 teaspoon each ground ginger and dried tarragon leaves, crumbled
4 dashes ground red (cayenne) pepper
2 tablespoons minced parsley

1. Heat oil in nonstick skillet until hot. Sauté shallots and sweet green pepper until wilted but not brown, stirring constantly.

2. Add rice to skillet. Stir and sauté for 1 minute.

3. Stir in balance of ingredients.

Bring to simmering point. Cover and simmer for 20 minutes, stirring once midway. Remove from heat. Let stand for 5 minutes. Fluff up with fork, sprinkle with parsley, and serve. All liquid will be absorbed and rice will be tender and moist.

YIELD: Serves 4

	CALORIES	SODIUM
Per serving:	161	33

Risotto, American Style (10 minutes)

Risotto, Italian rice, differs basically from rice of other nations in that each grain is tender, cooked through, and separate from all the others. In that respect, my rice is a risotto; but there's nothing else Italian about it. Expect, instead, a typical gourmet-cuisine-of-health dish studded with pleasant surprises, like grated orange rind, slivers of sweet red pepper, and tender mushroom slices.

Use iron skillet

1	tablespoon Italian olive oil	2	teaspoons Herb 'n Spice Mix (page 177)
½	medium sweet red pepper, cut into ¼-inch slivers	1	tablespoon grated orange rind (preferably from navel orange)
3	tablespoons minced shallots		
2	teaspoons minced garlic	1	tablespoon tarragon vinegar
¼	pound snow-white fresh mushrooms, rinsed, well dried, trimmed, and sliced	3	tablespoons dry white wine
		2	tablespoons minced fresh parsley
1¾	cups just-cooked brown rice or enriched white rice		

1. Heat oil in large well-seasoned iron skillet until hot. Sauté red pepper, shallots, garlic, and mushrooms until tender but not brown (about 4 minutes).

2. Add rice. Sprinkle with Herb 'n Spice Mix and orange rind. Stir to combine. Cook for 1 minute. Sprinkle with tarragon vinegar and cook for 30 seconds.

3. Stir in white wine and parsley. Cook briefly over medium-high heat until heated through. Transfer to warmed serving bowl, and serve at once.

YIELD: Serves 4

	CALORIES	SODIUM
Per serving:	161	12.5
With white rice	156	12.5

Sophisticated Bulgur (10 minutes)

Bulgur, a parboiled wheat product, acquires sophistication when it's furbished with snow-white mushrooms, tangy and minty savory, and an inspired sweet-and-tart mixture of Marsala and concentrated orange juice.

½ cup bulgur
¼ cup Marsala wine
1 tablespoon frozen orange juice concentrate (no sugar added)
2 tablespoons minced parsley
1 teaspoon minced dried onions
1 teaspoon Italian olive oil
2 large fresh mushrooms, washed, dried, trimmed, and coarsely chopped

1 teaspoon dried savory leaves, crushed
4 dashes ground red (cayenne) pepper
¾ cup water

1. Combine first 6 ingredients in heavy-bottomed stainless steel or enameled saucepan. Let stand for 5 minutes.
2. Add balance of ingredients. Bring to a boil. Cover and slow-boil for 10 minutes, stirring once midway. Stir. Re-cover and let stand for 5 minutes. All liquid will be absorbed and mixture will be moist and textured. Serve immediately.

YIELD: Serves 3

	CALORIES	SODIUM
Per serving:	149	5.5

Faster Recipes

Bright Green Peas with Orange-Hued Pimentos (15 minutes)

Combine sweet peas with the mildest of the peppers, pimentos (they're actually *ripe* green peppers, and hence on the sweet side), and balance with tangy herbs and the sting of ground red pepper (which is made from the hottest of chili peppers), and you have a dish of stimulating contrasts so typical of my cuisine. Extra added treat: those spiced mushrooms or duxelles.

Use nonstick skillet

1 pound fresh peas in the pod, shelled
1 teaspoon onion powder
2 teaspoons peanut or Italian olive oil
3 scallions, trimmed and minced
¼ pound snow-white fresh mushrooms, washed, dried, trimmed, and thinly sliced

1 teaspoon dried tarragon leaves, crumbled
¼ teaspoon ground ginger
1 tablespoon minced parsley
4 dashes ground red (cayenne) pepper
1 teaspoon fresh lemon juice
2 whole jarred pimentos (no salt added), drained and slivered

1. In small saucepan, cook peas in water to cover with onion powder until tender (about 8 minutes). Color should remain bright green. Drain.

2. Heat oil in nonstick skillet until hot. Sauté scallions for 1 minute. Add mushrooms and sauté over medium-high heat, stirring often, until wilted but not brown.

3. Sprinkle with tarragon, ginger, parsley, and ground red pepper, stirring to blend. Sprinkle with lemon juice.

4. Add peas. Sauté until heated through. Add pimentos and stir gently until heated and combined with all ingredients. Serve immediately.

YIELD: Serves 4

VARIATIONS:

1. Six ounces of frozen peas may be substituted for the fresh variety, but color will be sacrificed, and the sodium count will be higher (see statistics).

2. You may substitute ¼ cup Ready Duxelles (page 180) for fresh mushrooms. Just stir in during step 2 until heated through.

3. You may substitute 1 teaspoon Herb 'n Spice Mix (page 177) for tarragon, ginger, and ground red pepper.

	CALORIES	SODIUM
Per serving:	74	6
With Italian olive oil	No appreciable difference	
With frozen peas	74	61.5
With Ready Duxelles, subtract per serving	−5	−3
With Herb 'n Spice Mix	No appreciable difference	

Broccoli with Sesame Seed (15 minutes)

Cook broccoli to firm, crisp, jade-green perfection (that means rapidly; follow the instructions), add a bevy of contrasting flavors (nutmeg and ground red pepper, for example), and top with a sprinkling of delicious nutlike flavored toasted sesame seed—and let heaven wait.

Use nonstick skillet

- 2 tablespoons sesame seed (preferably unshelled)
- 2 cups fresh broccoli flowerets
- 2 teaspoons peanut oil
- 1 teaspoon sweet unsalted margarine-butter blend (page 182) or sweet unsalted corn oil margarine
- 3 tablespoons minced shallots
- ¾ teaspoon freshly grated nutmeg
- 6 dashes ground red (cayenne) pepper
- 2 teaspoons fresh lemon juice
- 2 tablespoons minced parsley
- 1 whole pimento, drained, and julienned

1. Sprinkle sesame seed into heated nonstick skillet and cook, shaking skillet often, until lightly toasted. Transfer to plate, spreading out in single layer, and let cool.

2. Drop broccoli into a saucepan of rapidly boiling water (or steam) and cook for 3 to 5 minutes (color should remain bright green). Pour into colander and drain.

3. Heat oil and margarine-butter blend in nonstick skillet until hot. Add broccoli and stir to coat. Then sprinkle with nutmeg and ground red pepper. Sauté while stirring for 1 minute. Remove from heat.

4. Sprinkle with lemon juice, parsley, and toasted seed, tossing gently to blend.

5. Turn onto warmed serving plate. Garnish with pimentos, and serve immediately.

YIELD: Serves 4

NOTE: Steps 1 and 2 may be completed well ahead of time and dish completed minutes before eating. Suggestion: In step 2, run cold water over 3-minute cooked broccoli in colander to stop cooking action.

	CALORIES	SODIUM
Per serving:	87	8.5
With margarine	No appreciable difference	

Vegetables and Dau Foo (15 minutes)

Dau Foo translates from the Chinese to "bean curd," that pallid, white and spongy, cheeselike edible derived from ground and jelled beans. Flavorless itself, its appeal to the taste buds depends entirely on how it's cooked and with what it's cooked. Here the "with what" is a spiced onion-y mix of sherry-tinged chicken stock studded with mushroom slices and slivers of red pepper. The "how it's cooked," is, naturally, in a wok—that oriental wonder that turns out savory crisp-tender delicacies with dazzling speed. (Even if you've never used a wok before, follow my instructions and you'll cook like a Chinese chef in just 15 minutes).

Use wok

1	tablespoon peanut oil
2	whole scallions, trimmed, cut diagonally into ½-inch slices
1	leek, white part only, trimmed, cut diagonally into ¼-inch slices
½	small sweet red pepper, seeded, and cut into ¼-inch slivers
¼	pound fresh mushrooms, rinsed, well dried, trimmed, and cut into ¼-inch slices

1½	teaspoons Herb 'n Spice Mix (page 177)
1	3-inch cake bean curd (about 4 ounces), dried, and cut into ½-inch chunks
¼	cup Delicious Chicken Stock (page 162)
1	teaspoon tomato paste (no salt added) (optional)
1	tablespoon dry sherry

1. Place wok on ring. Heat over high heat for 1½ minutes. Pour oil around rim of wok. When oil drips down, add scallions, leek, sweet red pepper, and mushrooms. Stir-fry for 1 minute.

2. Sprinkle with Herb 'n Spice Mix. Continue stir-frying for 1½ minutes.

3. Add bean curd and gently combine. Stir-fry for 1 minute.

4. Combine and blend stock with tomato paste. Pour around rim of wok. Bring to simmering point. Stir in sherry. Cover and cook for 1 minute. Serve immediately.

YIELD: Serves 3 (lunch) 2 (dinner)

NOTE: Recipe may be prepared in large nonstick skillet allowing a bit more cooking time over medium heat for each step. Texture will be less crisp-tender.

	CALORIES	SODIUM
Per serving, as luncheon dish:	124.5	17.5
Per serving, as main dish:	187	26
With tomato paste	No appreciable difference	

Name That Dish! (15 minutes)

As readers of my books know, I've invented a game called "Name That Dish!" Here's how to play it. Start with a commonplace ingredient, then, using your culinary skills, change it into an extraordinary delight. If the taster can identify the disguised ingredient after consuming up to a complete serving, you lose. But chances are you won't when you play the game with any of my Name That Dish! recipes. Here's a new one that confounded the most astute gastronomic sleuth I know (I'm married to him). He guessed—rice. (The correct answer is—sshhh!—bulgur.)

Use iron skillet

1 tablespoon peanut or Italian olive oil or a combination of both	½ cup raw bulgur
½ large sweet green pepper, seeded and coarsely chopped	1½ teaspoons Barbeque Spice Mix (page 178)
½ cup coarsely chopped onion	1 teaspoon wine vinegar
¼ pound fresh mushrooms, washed, dried, trimmed, and coarsely chopped	⅓ cup each Delicious Chicken Stock (page 162) and unsweetened pineapple juice
	1 tablespoon minced parsley

1. Measure oil into well-seasoned iron skillet. With a folded-over piece of waxed paper, spread oil across and around sides of skillet to coat. Then heat skillet to moderately hot. Spread green pepper and onion across skillet. Sauté until mixture begins to wilt (about 1½ minutes).

2. Add mushrooms, stir to combine, and sauté for 2 minutes, stirring constantly.

3. Stir in bulgur and cook for 1 minute. Then sprinkle with wine vinegar and spice mix, combining evenly.

4. Add stock, pineapple juice, and parsley. Bring to simmering point. Stir well to combine. Reduce heat to simmering. Cover tightly and simmer for 12 minutes, stirring and re-covering once midway.

5. Remove from heat. Let stand for 2 minutes. Fluff up with fork, and serve.

YIELD: Serves 4

VARIATIONS:

1. Sprinkle with 1 tablespoon grated part-skim mozzarella cheese per serving.

2. Add ½ cup dried crunchy, chopped mung bean sprouts to mixture at the end of step 4.

3. Stir in 4 ounces cooked cubed chicken, beef, or lamb to mixture at the end of step 4 and serve as main course.

	CALORIES	SODIUM
Per serving:	141.5	12
With mozzarella	162	82
With bean sprouts	147.5	12.5
With chicken*	170	25
With beef†	202.5	27
With lamb‡	194.5	32

*no salt added
†lean chuck, trimmed of separable fat, no salt added
‡Lean leg, trimmed of separable fat, no salt added

Bulgur Stuffing with Apricots (15 minutes)

The inspiration for this dish is Near Eastern, but the execution is American. Special treat: those irresistible pine nuts.

12 dried apricot halves, coarsely chopped
⅔ cup raw bulgur
2 slices Mixed Wheat Bread (page 171) or good quality commercial whole-wheat bread, toasted and cut into ½-inch cubes
1 leek, white part only, well washed and minced, or 1 medium onion, coarsely chopped

2 teaspoons minced garlic
2 tablespoons minced parsley or dill
1½ teaspoons Indian Spice Mix (page 178)
3 tablespoons Delicious Chicken Stock (page 162) or tomato juice (no salt added)
2 tablespoons pine nuts

1. Combine apricots and bulgur in small bowl. Pour boiling water to cover mixture. Let stand for 10 minutes.

2. In another bowl, combine bread with leek, garlic, parsley or dill, and Indian Spice Mix. Drain apricot-bulgur mixture and add to bowl. Stir in stock and pine nuts, blending with fork (do not mash).

YIELD: Serves 4; about 1¾ cups cooked stuffing; enough to stuff a 3-pound broiling chicken or 3 Cornish hens

	CALORIES	SODIUM
Per serving:	179	11.5
With commercial whole-wheat bread	179	80
With onion	No appreciable difference	
With dill	No appreciable difference	
With tomato juice	179	6.5

Steamed Couscous in Red Wine (15 minutes)

Use supermarket couscous, but don't follow the instructions on the box (unless you want a sticky mess). Do follow the instructions in this recipe, and you'll discover a new exciting alternate to potatoes, rice, and pasta. Long a favorite in Algeria, Tunisia, and Morocco, couscous is cracked semolina wheat steamed over water or a stock. Here, I use my chicken stock augmented with red wine.

Use steamer and cotton cheesecloth

½ cup precooked couscous
About ⅔ cup warmed Delicious
    Chicken Stock (page 162)

⅓ cup dry red wine

1. Place couscous in small bowl. Moisten by sprinkling with ⅓ cup warmed stock, separating grains with fork. Let stand for 2 minutes (no longer or it will harden). Combine balance of stock with wine.

2. Fill steamer with water and bring to boil. Line perforated section with a piece of moistened cotton cheese-cloth. Spoon moistened couscous onto cheesecloth. Sprinkle with ¼ cup stock-wine mixture, separating grains with fork. Cover tightly and steam for 15 to 20 minutes, sprinkling with spoonfuls of stock-wine mixture every 5 minutes while fluffing with fork. Finished couscous will be tender, moist, and nonsticky.

YIELD: Serves 4

NOTE: I've allowed flexibility of 5 minutes' cooking time contingent upon the efficiency of steamer. For directions on devising your own steamer, see *Francine Prince's New Gourmet Recipes for Dieters.*

VARIATIONS:
1. Substitute ⅓ cup dry white wine for red wine.
2. Substitute apple juice (no sugar added) for red wine.
3. Prepare couscous with 1 cup stock, eliminating wine.

	CALORIES	SODIUM
Per serving:	136.5	21
With white wine	No appreciable difference	
With apple juice	159.5	20.5
With 1 cup stock	140.5	45.5

Fast Recipes

Marvelous Turnips and Carrot Stew (20 minutes)

This is good, hearty, no-nonsense, stick-to-the ribs food. But dig the gourmet overtones: sherry, leeks, fresh dill, and my special mixtures of herbs and spices. Marvelous!

Use pressure cooker

1 tablespoon sweet unsalted margarine-butter blend (page 182)
1 leek, well washed, white part only, coarsely chopped
4 medium carrots, peeled and diced
2 white turnips (about ¾ pound), peeled, trimmed, and diced

2 teaspoons Herb 'n Spice Mix (page 177)
⅓ cup Delicious Chicken Stock (page 162)
¼ cup dry sherry
2 tablespoons just-snipped fresh dill

1. Heat margarine-butter blend in pressure cooker until melted but not brown. Add leek and sauté until wilted, stirring constantly (about 3 minutes).

2. Add carrots and turnips. Sprinkle with Herb 'n Spice Mix. Sauté for 2 minutes.

3. Stir in stock, sherry, and dill. Bring to simmering point. Cover securely. Place pressure regulator on vent pipe and cook for 4 minutes with pressure regulator rocking slowly. Cool at once under cold running water, and serve.

YIELD: Serves 4

VARIATIONS:
1. Thicken sauce lightly. Place pot without cover back on stove after completion of step 3. Slowly dribble in 1½ teaspoons arrowroot flour that has been dissolved in 2 teaspoons water. Cook for 1 minute, and serve.

2. Convert to puree. Complete recipe through step 3. Turn into food processor work bowl. Process for 10 seconds. Scrape down sides of bowl. Turn processor on/off several times until desired texture is reached. Finished puree should be textured and not oversmooth.

	CALORIES	SODIUM
Per serving:	89.5	67.5
With arrowroot flour	93	68

Linguine with No-Cook Watercress Sauce

(20 minutes)

Serve it tepid with the quick food-processored sauce. An adventure for pasta lovers.

Use food processor

1 cup each tightly packed parsley flowerets and watercress leaves, well washed and dried
6 large Boston lettuce leaves, washed, dried, tough center removed
3 large shallots, peeled and quartered
1 small onion, peeled, cut into 1-inch chunks

3 tablespoons Italian olive oil
1 tablespoon wine vinegar
1 teaspoon each garlic powder and no-fat Sap Sago cheese (page 182)
⅓ cup tomato juice (no salt added)
4 ounces thin linguine (see Notes 1 and 4)

1. Fit food processor with steel blade. In work bowl combine first 4 listed ingredients. Turn processor on/off 3 times. Scrape down sides of bowl.
2. Pour olive oil over mixture in circular motion. Sprinkle with vinegar, garlic powder, and cheese. Turn processor on and puree for 5 seconds.

3. With machine running pour tomato juice through feed tube.
4. Measure out ¾ cup of sauce. Spoon over just-cooked, well-drained linguine. Stir briefly. Let stand uncovered for 3 minutes. Stir again and serve at room temperature.

YIELD: Serves 6 (side dish); sauce 1½ cups

NOTES:

1. To conserve time, bring pot of water to simmering point before preparing sauce. Then start to cook linguine after sauce ingredients are assembled in food processor.

2. To serve 4 as a main course, cook 8 ounces of linguine and use all of sauce. Nutritional statistics will double.

3. Serve balance of sauce over cold vegetables, fish, poultry, meat or hard-cooked eggs.

4. Ronzoni's Capellini 11 is a thin macaroni that cooks in just 5 minutes.

	CALORIES	SODIUM
Per serving:	154	23

Breakfast and Luncheon Dishes

"Most breakfast skippers are chronic overeaters." That's a quote from the U.S. Department of Agriculture's publication *Foods*. So dieting becomes much easier when you acquire the breakfast habit. And the easiest way to do it is with *fast, faster, fastest* breakfasts (that takes care of your "I'm-in-a-hurry" excuse) that are out of the commonplace (that takes care of your "Oh-breakfasts are-so-boring" alibi) and that are ummm-good delicious (and that takes care of your "Breakfast-is-Dullsville" copout).

Instructions to the reader: Substitute "lunch" for "breakfast" in the preceding paragraph, and repeat.

Breakfast Dishes

Fastest Recipes

High-Style Granola (10 minutes)

Use nonstick skillet

1 cup raw old-fashioned rolled oats
¼ cup The Healthy Sweetener (page 182)
2 tablespoons date sugar (page 182)
2 tablespoons toasted wheat germ (no sugar added)
½ shredded wheat biscuit, crumbled

1 tablespoon unprocessed bran
1 teaspoon each ground cinnamon and coriander
2 tablespoons finely chopped walnuts
2 tablespoons dark seedless raisins

1. Lightly toast rolled oats in heated nonstick skillet, turning frequently with spatula, and taking care not to burn (about 3 minutes). Transfer to bowl.

2. Stir in balance of ingredients in listed order. Store tightly closed in a cool dry place.

YIELD: 8 servings (¼ cup each)

NOTE: Recipe may be doubled successfully.

	CALORIES	SODIUM
Per serving:	89	2

Festive Breakfast Apricots (10 minutes)

1   11-ounce box medium dried apricots
1½   cups apple juice (no sugar added)
½   teaspoon finely grated lemon rind

½   teaspoon ground cinnamon
¼   teaspoon each freshly grated nutmeg and ground cardamom

1. Combine all ingredients in 1½-quart stainless-steel or enameled saucepan. Bring to a boil. Reduce heat to simmering. Cover and simmer for 13 minutes.

2. Remove from heat. Let stand, partially covered, until cooled. Most of liquid will be absorbed. Serve warm or chilled *au naturel*.

YIELD: 4

VARIATION:

1. This recipe has a delicate tart flavor. If you prefer a sweeter taste, stir in 1 tablespoon honey at end of step 2 or 1 packet (1 gram) Equal after apricots have cooled for 10 minutes.

2. Serve with 1 portion Whipped Orange Topping (page 161) or 2 tablespoons Creamy Yogurt Topping (page 162).

	CALORIES	SODIUM
Per serving:	130.5	11
With honey	137	11
With Equal	No appreciable difference	
With Whipped Orange Topping	160.5	27.5
With Creamy Yogurt Topping	145.5	16.5

Banana Hotcake (10 minutes)

Use iron skillet

Preheat oven to 425°F

½ cup unbleached flour
½ teaspoon baking powder
½ teaspoon ground cinnamon
¼ teaspoon freshly grated nutmeg
¼ cup High-Style Granola (page 113), pulverized in food blender
2 large eggs (use 1 yolk and 2 whites)
1 ripe medium banana, mashed (¼ cup)

½ cup nonfat liquid milk
½ teaspoon pure vanilla extract
1 tablespoon plus 2 teaspoons sweet unsalted margarine-butter blend (page 182) or sweet unsalted corn oil margarine
1 1-gram packet Equal (optional)

1. Sift flour, baking powder, and spices into mixing bowl. Stir in granola.

2. In another bowl, whisk eggs until well blended. Combine mashed banana with milk. Whisk into eggs. Stir in vanilla.

3. Gradually add egg mixture to dry ingredients, stirring with wooden spoon until all flour is well moistened.

4. Heat 1 tablespoon margarine-butter blend or margarine in well-seasoned 10-inch iron skillet until melted and bubbly. Pour batter into skillet, tilting from side to side to evenly distribute. Transfer skillet to preheated oven and bake for 15 minutes.

5. While hotcake is baking, melt 2 teaspoons shortening over a pot of simmering water. Stir in Equal and dissolve. When hotcake is fully baked, dip pastry brush in melted mixture and coat top. Cut into 8 wedges, and serve immediately.

YIELD: Serves 4

Per serving:

	CALORIES	SODIUM
	177	95

Mushroom Omelette (10 minutes)

Lovely for lunch, too.

Use nonstick skillet

3 eggs (use 1 yolk, 3 whites)
2 teaspoons minced dried onions
2 tablespoons evaporated skim milk
3 dashes ground red (cayenne) pepper
1 teaspoon peanut oil or Italian olive oil

3 large snow-white fresh mushrooms, washed, dried, trimmed, and sliced
½ teaspoon curry powder (no salt or pepper added)
1 tablespoon minced fresh dill
Sprinkle (about ⅛ teaspoon) tarragon vinegar

1. In small bowl, combine and blend first 4 ingredients. Set aside.
2. Measure oil into nonstick skillet. With folded-over piece of waxed paper, spread oil across and around sides of skillet to coat. Then heat skillet. Sauté mushrooms for 3 minutes over medium-high heat (do not brown) stirring constantly. Sprinkle with curry powder. Stir.
3. Whisk egg mixture briefly. Pour over mushrooms. Quickly stir mixture.

Then cook for 30 seconds. Tilt pan in a complete circle so that residue will adhere to sides of skillet. Cook until lightly browned on one side only (center should remain moist). Sprinkle with dill.
4. Slide onto warmed dish. Flip half over. Cut into 2 servings. Sprinkle with vinegar, and serve immediately.

YIELD: Serves 2

Per serving:
With Italian
olive oil

CALORIES
99.5

SODIUM
121

No appreciable difference

Ricotta Cheese Omelette (10 minutes)

A good lunch, too.

Use nonstick skillet

3 eggs (use 1 yolk, 3 whites)
1 tablespoon evaporated skim milk
½ teaspoon Indian Spice Mix (page 178)
1 tablespoon minced parsley
1 tablespoon Ready Duxelles (page 180)

1 teaspoon peanut oil or Italian olive oil
1 tablespoon minced shallot
3 tablespoons part-skim ricotta cheese

1. In small bowl, combine and blend first 5 ingredients. Set aside.

2. Heat oil in nonstick skillet until hot. Spread shallot across skillet. Whisk egg mixture briefly. Pour over shallot. Cook for 30 seconds. Then tilt pan in a complete circle so that residue will adhere to sides of skillet.

When mixture begins to congeal in center, gently spread ricotta cheese across omelette. Reduce heat and cook until cheese is heated through and omelette is lightly browned. (Center should remain moist.)

3. Slide onto warmed dish. Carefully fold half over. Cut into 2 servings.

YIELD: Serves 2

Per serving:
With Italian olive oil

	CALORIES	SODIUM
	121	96.5
	No appreciable difference	

Prune Butter (10 minutes)

Use food mill

1   8-ounce can moist pitted prunes
¼ cup each apple juice (no sugar added) and sweet Madeira wine (Malmsey)
4   whole cloves

¼ teaspoon each ground cardamom and freshly grated nutmeg
½ teaspoon ground cinnamon
1   slice orange

1. Combine all ingredients in small heavy-bottomed saucepan. Bring to simmering point. Cover and simmer for 7 minutes. Stir. Remove from heat. Let stand, uncovered, for 5 minutes. Discard orange slices.

2. Puree through food mill. Store in glass jar. Serve chilled.

YIELD: Scant cup

NOTE: I prefer the canned variety of dried prunes because there are no preservatives added, and they cook to tenderness rapidly.

	CALORIES	SODIUM
Per tablespoon:	22	1

Faster Recipes

Banana-Bran Muffins (15 minutes)

Preheat oven to 400°F

⅓ cup The Healthy Sweetener (see Note)
½ cup each buttermilk (no salt added) and apple juice (no sugar added)
¼ cup whole-wheat flour (preferably stone ground)
1½ cups unbleached flour
3 teaspoons ground ginger
2 teaspoons baking powder

1 egg
2 tablespoons honey (optional)
2 tablespoons sweet unsalted margarine-butter blend (page 182), melted, plus ½ teaspoon for pans
½ cup mashed banana (about 1 small banana)
1 tablespoon finely grated orange rind (preferably from navel orange)

1. Place The Healthy Sweetener in small bowl. Combine buttermilk and apple juice in saucepan and heat until just warm. Pour over bran mixture and stir. Set aside.

2. Sift flours, ginger, and baking powder into large mixing bowl.

3. In cup, beat egg, honey, and melted margarine-butter blend with a fork until smooth. Stir in mashed banana.

4. Add banana mixture to sifted dry ingredients. Stir with wooden spoon.

Then stir in bran-milk mixture and orange rind. Do not beat; mixture will be thick and textured.

5. Three-quarter fill 12 small lightly greased muffin cups. Bake in center section of preheated oven for about 15 minutes. Muffins should be lightly browned and recede from sides of cups when fully baked. Let cool on rack in pan for 5 minutes. Then loosen with blunt knife and remove from pans. Serve warm.

YIELD: 12 muffins

NOTE: The Healthy Sweetener is a sweet-tasting mixture of toasted bran and ground dried dates. It's available in most supermarkets and specialty stores or by mail (see page 182 for details).

	CALORIES	SODIUM
Per muffin:	123	52
With honey	133.5	52

New French Toast with Fruit Sauce (15 minutes)

Use food blender

Use nonstick skillet

3   eggs (use 1 egg yolk and 3 egg whites)
¼   cup each evaporated skim milk and pineapple juice (no sugar added)
½   teaspoon Indian Spice Mix (page 178)
4   slices Orange Rye Loaf (page 176), or 4 thin slices good quality light-textured commercial bread
½   16-ounce can apricot halves, packed in water (no sugar added), drained

¼   cup pineapple juice (no sugar added)
8   pineapple chunks (about ⅓ cup) (no sugar added)
¼   teaspoon each freshly grated nutmeg and ground cinnamon
1   teaspoon honey (optional)
2   teaspoons sweet unsalted margarine-butter blend (page 182) or sweet unsalted corn oil margarine

1. In large bowl, combine and beat first 3 ingredients until blended. Add bread, and soak until most of liquid is absorbed.

2. Meanwhile, prepare sauce by combining apricots, pineapple juice, pineapple chunks, spices, and honey in blender. Blend on high speed for 30 seconds. Pour into saucepan. Place over low heat.

3. Heat 1 teaspoon margarine-butter blend in large nonstick skillet until melted and hot, taking care not to burn. Sauté bread over medium-high heat until brown. Add balance of shortening (1 teaspoon) to skillet. When it melts, turn bread and sauté until browned.

4. Serve on warmed individual plates. Pour warmed sauce into sauceboat and serve with toast.

YIELD: Serves 4

	CALORIES	SODIUM
Toast, per serving using orange loaf:	93	68
With commercial bread	110	179.5
With honey, add	+8.5	+0
Sauce, per tablespoon:	14	0

Luncheon Dishes

Fastest Recipes

Baked Open-Faced Egg Salad Sandwich (10 minutes)

Preheat oven to 450°F

3 hard-cooked eggs (use 1 yolk, 3 whites), warm
2 tablespoons Zesty Salad Dressing (page 135)
½ teaspoon each tomato paste (no salt added) and prepared Dijon mustard (no salt added)
1 teaspoon Herb 'n Spice Mix (page 177)
3 tablespoons minced onion

3 tablespoons finely grated part-skim mozzarella cheese
1 tablespoon minced fresh parsley, mint, or dill
3 slices Mixed Wheat Bread or Delicate Textured Loaf (pages 173 and 171), or good quality thin-sliced commercial whole-wheat bread
Radish flowerets

1. In a small bowl, finely mash eggs. Combine and blend salad dressing with tomato paste, mustard, and Herb 'n Spice Mix. Stir into eggs. Then stir in onion, mozzarella, cheese, and parsley.

2. Spread equal amounts of salad on 3 slices of bread.

3. Place in baking pan and bake in preheated oven for 7 to 10 minutes. Cheese should be melted and salad heated through. Serve hot, garnished with radishes.

YIELD: Serves 3

Per serving:	CALORIES	SODIUM
With Mixed Wheat Bread	153	85.5
With Delicate Textured Loaf	159	91
With commercial whole-wheat bread	153	222
With mint or dill	No appreciable difference	

New and Light-Tasting Egg Salad (10 minutes)

2 ounces frozen Chinese pea pods (see Note)
3 hard-cooked eggs (use 3 whites, 1 yolk)
1 teaspoon tarragon vinegar
2 tablespoons each coarsely grated carrot and onion

4 teaspoons Zesty Salad Dressing (page 135)
1 teaspoon Herb 'n Spice Mix or Indian Spice Mix (pages 177 or 178)
2 teaspoons low-fat plain yogurt
1 tablespoon minced fresh parsley, tarragon, or mint

1. Drop frozen Chinese pea pods in a pot of rapidly boiling water. Cook for 15 seconds. Drain. Cool under cold running water. Pat dry with paper toweling and coarsely chop.
2. In bowl, mash eggs. Stir in vinegar. Then add chopped pea pods, carrot, and onion.
3. In cup, combine Zesty Salad Dressing with Herb 'n Spice Mix. Add to salad, stirring to blend. Then stir in yogurt and parsley. Serve immediately.

YIELD: Serves 2

NOTE: Frozen Chinese pea pods are a wonderful convenience item. They're generally the small variety, are trimmed and frozen in 6-ounce boxes. Blanche the whole box; use one third for this quick recipe and reserve balance in refrigerator for another recipe.

VARIATIONS:
1. Eliminate carrot and substitute 2 whole pimentos (well drained and coarsely chopped) for pea pods. Mixture will be more spreadable than the original recipe.
2. Add 2 tablespoons cooled cooked rice to mixture at end of step 2 in original recipe or in variation above, increasing spice mix by ½ teaspoon.

	CALORIES	SODIUM
Per serving:	118.5	105.5
With Indian Spice Mix, tarragon, mint	No appreciable difference	
Variation 1	108.5	99
Variation 2	123.5	106

Luncheon Pizza (10 minutes)

Preheat oven to 400°F

½ teaspoon each prepared Dijon mustard and tomato paste (no salt added)

¼ teaspoon Herb 'n Spice Mix (page 177) or curry powder (no salt added)

2 slices thin-sliced good quality commercial rye or whole-wheat bread or any of my breads (pages 171—176)

2 ounces roast skinned chicken, light meat, ¼ inch thick

1 tablespoon minced fresh dill or parsley

2 ounces thin-sliced part-skim mozzarella cheese

1. Combine mustard with tomato paste and Herb 'n Spice Mix or curry powder. Spread equal amounts on each slice bread.

2. Lay chicken slices on mixture. Sprinkle with one half of parsley, pressing into chicken.

3. Cover chicken with cheese slices. Bake in preheated oven for 8 to 10 minutes, or until cheese is completely melted and starts to turn a golden brown. Serve immediately.

YIELD: Serves 2

VARIATIONS:

1. Use 2 ounces thinly sliced cooked lean lamb or beef in place of chicken.

2. Sprinkle 2 teaspoons minced shallots on mustard mixture before continuing with recipe.

	CALORIES	SODIUM
Per serving:		
With commercial rye bread	176.5	289.5
With commercial whole-wheat bread	176.5	289.5
With Onion Rye Loaves	185	155
With Orange Rye Loaves	160	156
With Mixed Wheat Bread	176.5	153
With Delicate Textured Bread	173	158
With curry powder, parsley, shallots	No appreciable difference	
With lamb (leg), add	+45.5	+5
With beef (round steak), add	+30	+9

Tomato Omelette with Vegetables (10 minutes)

Use nonstick skillet

3   eggs (use 1 yolk, 3 whites)
2   teaspoons minced dried onions
2   tablespoons evaporated skim milk
1   teaspoon dried basil leaves, crumbled
3   dashes ground red (cayenne) pepper

3   tablespoons tomato juice (no salt added)
1   teaspoon peanut oil or Italian olive oil
2   scallions, coarsely chopped
½   small sweet green or red pepper, coarsely chopped or julienned

1. In small bowl, combine and blend first 6 ingredients. Set aside.

2. Heat oil in nonstick skillet until hot. Sauté scallions and sweet pepper over medium-high heat for 3 minutes, turning constantly. Whisk egg mixture briefly. Pour over sautéed mixture. Quickly stir. Then cook for 30 seconds.

Tilt pan in a complete circle so that residue will adhere to sides of skillet. Cook until lightly browned on one side only (the center should remain moist).

3. Slide onto warmed dish. Flip half over. Cut omelette in half, and serve immediately.

YIELD: Serves 2

	CALORIES	SODIUM
Per serving:	125.5	112
With Italian olive oil	No appreciable difference	
With red pepper	No appreciable difference	

Faster Recipes

Zucchini Egg Salad (15 minutes)

Use food processor

1   small onion, peeled and quartered
½   cup loosely packed just-snipped dill and parsley flowerets
1   small zucchini (about ¼ pound), trimmed, scrubbed and diced into ½-inch pieces
3   hard-cooked eggs (use 1 yolk, 3 whites)
½   teaspoon Indian Spice Mix (page 178)

3   dashes ground red (cayenne) pepper
1½ teaspoons frozen orange juice concentrate (no sugar added)
2   tablespoons part-skim ricotta cheese
2   tablespoons Zesty Salad Dressing (page 135)
    Bibb or Boston lettuce cups
    Cherry tomatoes (3 per serving)

1. Fit food processor with steel blade. Place onion, dill, and parsley in work bowl. Process on/off 4 times. Scrape down sides of bowl. Add zucchini. Process on/off 4 times. Transfer mixture to bowl.

2. To work bowl add eggs, spices, and orange juice concentrate. Process on/off twice. Transfer to bowl, stirring to blend.

3. Fold in cheese and salad dressing (do not mash).

4. Arrange lettuce cups on 3 salad plates. Spoon with equal amounts of salad. Garnish with cherry tomatoes.

YIELD: Serves 2 or 3

NOTE: Mixture may be prepared by hand, if desired. Here's how: Mince onion and fresh herbs. Coarsely grate zucchini. Fork-mash egg with spices and orange juice concentrate. Stir in cheese and salad dressing. Add 5 minutes to preparation time.

	CALORIES	SODIUM
Per serving, serves 2:	183.5	110
Per serving, serves 3:	125.5	74

Orange Rice Salad (15 minutes)

¾ cup raw enriched rice
6 tablespoons Orange Salad Dressing (page 136)
2 tablespoons minced parsley
3 scallions, including tender green part, trimmed and thinly sliced
¼ pound snow-white fresh mushrooms, washed, dried, trimmed, halved, and thinly sliced

1 medium navel orange, peeled, sliced, and cut into 1-inch chunks
12 large crisp romaine lettuce leaves, rinsed, well dried, tough center sections removed
6 tablespoons part-skim ricotta cheese (see Note)

1. Add rice to large pot of boiling water. Boil for 12 minutes. Drain well. Transfer to bowl. Stir in 2 tablespoons Orange Salad Dressing. Cover with plastic wrap. Place in freezer and chill for 30 minutes.

2. Add parsley, scallions, and mushrooms to bowl. Fold in balance of salad dressing (4 tablespoons). Then gently stir in orange chunks.

3. Arrange lettuce leaves on 6 serving plates. Spoon with salad. Top with cheese and serve.

YIELD: Serves 6 or 8; about 2 cups

NOTE: To serve 8, use 8 tablespoons ricotta cheese.

	CALORIES	SODIUM
Serves 6, per serving:	178	12.5
Serves 8, per serving:	138.5	9

Exotic Mushrooms on Toast (15 minutes)

Two different techniques (one in this recipe, the other in the next) produce two different flavors.

Use nonstick skillet

1 tablespoon peanut oil

2 tablespoons minced shallots

½ pound snow-white fresh mushrooms, washed, dried, trimmed, and coarsely chopped

1¼ teaspoons Indian Spice Mix (page 178)

½ cup each Delicious Chicken Stock (page 162) and evaporated skim milk

1 tablespoon arrowroot flour dissolved in 1 tablespoon water

4 slices just-toasted Delicate Textured Loaf or Mixed Wheat Bread (pages 171 or 173) or thin-sliced good quality commercial whole-wheat bread

2 tablespoons minced parsley

1. Heat oil in nonstick skillet until hot. Sauté shallots and mushrooms for 2 minutes, stirring often. Sprinkle with Indian Spice Mix and continue to sauté and stir for 2 minutes.

2. Add stock. Bring to simmering point. Simmer, uncovered, for 1 minute.

3. Slowly pour in evaporated skim milk. Cook over low heat until mixture is just under simmering point. Remove from heat.

4. Whisk in arrowroot mixture (it will thicken instantly). Return skillet to low heat and cook for 1 minute while whisking.

5. Spoon over just-toasted bread. Sprinkle with parsley and serve immediately.

YIELD: Serves 4

VARIATIONS: Instead of toast, serve over just-cooked rice (about ⅓ cup per portion) or just-cooked thin spaghetti (about ½ cup per portion).

Per serving:	CALORIES	SODIUM
With Delicate Textured Loaf	139.5	48.5
With Mixed Wheat Bread	143	43.5
With commercial whole-wheat bread	143	180
With just-cooked rice	143.5	42
With just-cooked thin spaghetti	173.5	41.5

Spicy Mushrooms on Toast (15 minutes)

½ pound snow-white fresh mushrooms, washed, trimmed, and coarsely chopped
½ cup Delicious Chicken Stock (page 162) or water
1 teaspoon frozen orange juice concentrate (no sugar added)
1 tablespoon dry sherry
1 tablespoon peanut oil
2 tablespoons minced shallots

1½ teaspoons Herb 'n Spice Mix (page 177)
½ cup nonfat liquid milk
1 tablespoon arrowroot flour dissolved in 1 tablespoon water
4 slices just-toasted Delicate Textured Loaf or Mixed Wheat Bread (pages 171 or 173) or commercial whole-wheat bread
1 tablespoon minced chives

1. In heavy-bottomed saucepan, combine first 4 ingredients. Bring to a boil. Reduce heat to simmering. Partially cover and simmer for 5 minutes. Drain mushrooms, reserving liquid. There should be ¾ cup cooking liquid. If less, add stock or water to increase measurement to ¾ cup. Set aside. Wipe out saucepan.

2. Heat oil in saucepan until hot. Sauté shallots until translucent, stirring often, taking care not to brown (about 3 minutes).

3. Add drained mushrooms. Sauté for 1 minute. Sprinkle with Herb 'n Spice Mix, stirring to blend.

4. Add reserved cooking liquid. Simmer for 1 minute. Then add nonfat milk and simmer for 1 minute.

5. Stir in arrowroot flour mixture. Sauce will thicken rapidly. Continue to simmer for 1 minute.

6. Spoon over just-toasted bread. Sprinkle with chives and serve immediately.

YIELD: Serves 4

VARIATIONS: Instead of toast, serve over just-cooked rice (about ⅓ cup per portion) or just-cooked thin spaghetti (about ½ cup per portion).

	CALORIES	SODIUM
Per serving:		
With Delicate Textured Loaf	136.5	46
With Mixed Wheat Bread	140	41
With commercial whole-wheat bread	140	177.5
With just-cooked rice	141	39.5
With just-cooked thin spaghetti	175	39

The Quarter-Pound Lunch (15 minutes)

Do you ever, as I do, find yourself with a little broccoli, a bit of zucchini, two or three mushrooms, a tomato . . . odds and ends of foods? Not any single odd or end can make a dish, no less a meal. But artfully blend the single units together in quarter-pound portions, as I've done here, and you have a delectable *complete* lunch for two as fulfilling as it is filling. (Your copious portion of high-fiber foods weighs much more than a quarter of a pound.)

Use wok (optional)

1   tablespoon peanut oil
2   teaspoons minced garlic
¼   pound onion, peeled and thinly sliced
¼   cup frozen whole kernel corn
¼   pound broccoli flowerets from 1 broccoli stalk
¼   pound zucchini, well scrubbed and sliced into ¼-inch pieces
¼   pound snow-white fresh mushrooms, washed, dried, trimmed, and thickly sliced

1½   teaspoons Indian Spice Mix (page 178)
¼   pound fresh tomato, cored and seeded
¼   cup Delicious Chicken Stock (page 162)
1   teaspoon tomato paste (no salt added)
2   tablespoons dry sherry
¼   cup grated part-skim mozzarella cheese

1. Place wok on ring. Heat over high heat for 1½ minutes. Pour oil around rim of wok. When oil drips down, add garlic and onion. Stir-fry for 1 minute. Add corn. Stir-fry for 30 seconds.

2. Add broccoli, zucchini, and mushrooms. Sprinkle with Indian Spice Mix. Stir-fry for 2 minutes, combining all ingredients well.

3. Stir in tomato. Stir-fry for 1 minute.

4. In cup, combine stock with tomato paste and sherry, beating with fork to blend. Pour around rim of wok. Stir in cheese. Cover and cook for 1½ minutes. Uncover, and cook for 30 seconds. Serve immediately

YIELD: Serves 2

VARIATIONS:

1. Serve over just-cooked rice, allowing ⅓ cup rice per portion.
2. If desired, lightly thicken sauce by dissolving 1½ teaspoons cornstarch in 2 teaspoons water, and pouring around sides of wok toward the end of step 4.

NOTE: Recipe may also be prepared in a large well-seasoned iron skillet allowing a bit more time for each sequence. Results will be tasty but not as crisp-tender.

	CALORIES	SODIUM
Per serving:	209	118
With rice	271	119
With cornstarch	278.5	119

Fast Recipe

Puffy Potato Cakes (20 minutes)

Use nonstick skillet

⅓ cup each evaporated skim milk and water
1 egg
2 teaspoons minced dried onions
¾ cup unbleached flour
2 teaspoons baking powder
1 teaspoon curry powder (no salt or pepper added)
½ teaspoon dried tarragon leaves, crumbled

½ cup just-grated Idaho or russet potato
2 tablespoons low-fat plain yogurt
1 teaspoon sweet unsalted margarine-butter blend (page 182), melted
¾ teaspoon peanut oil (or less)

1. In small bowl, whisk skim milk, water, and egg until well blended. Stir in dried onions. Set aside.

2. Sift flour and baking powder into large bowl. Stir in curry powder and tarragon leaves.

3. Beat liquid mixture into dry ingredients until all liquid is absorbed and mixture is smooth.

4. Stir in potatoes; then stir in yogurt and melted margarine-butter blend.

5. Prepare 3-inch potato cakes in three batches in large nonstick skillet. Spread ¼ teaspoon oil across skillet. Heat over medium heat until a drop of water bounces off. Drop batter by tablespoonfuls into skillet. Cook for 3 minutes or until bottom of cakes are browned and tops are bubbly. Turn. Cook until puffed up and browned (about 3 minutes). Transfer to warmed plate and serve hot out of the skillet.

YIELD: 15 or 16 potato cakes

	CALORIES	SODIUM
Per potato cake, 16 cakes:	41	40
Per potato cake, 15 cakes:	44	42.5
With russet potato	No appreciable difference	

Salads and Salad Dressings

Salad-sameness is giving salads a bad name. So I've started a one-woman campaign to propel salads, and their dressings, into the culinary avant garde Sample a few titles—Witloof Salad, Orange Salad Dressing, Yam Salad, Mint Salad Dressing—and you'll get the idea. Sample the salads *cum* dressings themselves, and you'll never yawn again when the salad course comes around.

Salads

Fastest Recipes

Witloof Salad (10 minutes)

As if you didn't know—witloof is the Belgian endive.

1 large Belgian endive, trimmed, rinsed, well dried, and cut into ¼-inch slices (see Note, page 165)

3 large snow-white crisp fresh mushrooms, rinsed, dried, trimmed and cut into ¼-inch slices

2 medium carrots, peeled and coarsely grated

3 tablespoons minced fresh parsley

2 tablespoons tarragon vinegar

2 tablespoons Zesty Salad Dressing (page 135)

1 tablespoon low-fat plain yogurt

1. Combine first 4 ingredients in salad bowl. Toss.

2. Sprinkle with tarragon vinegar. Toss again. Let stand for 1 minute.

3. Stir in salad dressing. Then stir in yogurt. Let stand for 5 minutes. Stir and serve.

YIELD: Serves 4

Per serving:

	CALORIES	SODIUM
	53	30

Crispy Green Salad with Mint (10 minutes)

10 red-leaf lettuce leaves (about ½ head)
10 inner chicory leaves
1 medium red onion, peeled and thinly sliced
¼ pound fresh mushrooms, washed, dried, trimmed, and sliced
½ cup loosely packed fresh mint leaves, coarsely chopped

2 tablespoons each tarragon vinegar, wine vinegar, apple juice (no sugar added), and tomato puree (no salt added)
2 tablespoons extra virgin olive oil (See Note, page 36)
4 dashes ground red (cayenne) pepper

1. Wash lettuce and chicory leaves. Dry thoroughly on paper toweling. Cut away tough inner sections of each leaf. Break (do not cut) into bite-size pieces. Place in large bowl.

2. Add onion, mushrooms, and mint to bowl. Toss.

3. Prepare dressing just before serving. In jar, combine vinegars, apple juice, tomato puree, olive oil, and ground red pepper. Shake well. Pour over salad. Toss gently.

YIELD: Serves 4

Per serving:

	CALORIES	SODIUM
	100	21

Faster Recipes

Orange Chicken Salad (15 minutes)

3 cups cooked skinned chicken, cut into ½-inch chunks
1 small sweet red pepper, seeded, and cut into ¼-inch slivers
2 medium Belgian endives, trimmed and cut into ¼-inch slices
4 medium scallions, including green part, trimmed, and cut diagonally into ½-inch slices
¼ pound snow-white fresh mushrooms, washed, well dried, and thinly sliced

1 recipe Orange Salad Dressing (page 136)
2 tablespoons pine nuts lightly toasted in nonstick skillet
4 large romaine lettuce leaves, tough centers removed
1 medium navel orange, scored and thinly sliced, each slice cut in half

1. Combine first 5 ingredients in large salad bowl. Toss gently to combine.

2. Pour salad dressing over mixture, stirring to coat. Cover and refrigerate for 30 minutes. Then add pine nuts and toss.

3. Arrange lettuce leaves on decorative serving platter. Spoon salad over leaves and surround with orange slices.

YIELD: Serves 6

	CALORIES	SODIUM
Per serving:	184	22

New Coleslaw (15 minutes)

Use food processor

1 1-pound head crisp green cabbage (you will need 5 cups shredded cabbage)
1 zucchini, peeled and trimmed
1 medium carrot, scrubbed
1 medium onion, peeled
2 tablespoons fresh lemon juice
⅓ cup fresh orange juice

1 tablespoon apple cider vinegar
½ teaspoon freshly grated nutmeg
2 tablespoons minced fresh tarragon, or 1 teaspoon dried tarragon leaves, crumbled
1 tablespoon honey, or 1 packet Equal (1 gram)
1 cup buttermilk (no salt added)

1. Fit food processor with shredding disc. Shred first 4 ingredients. Transfer to large bowl. Toss.

2. Combine lemon juice, orange juice, and cider vinegar. Pour over vegetables. Sprinkle with nutmeg and tarragon. Toss to blend.

3. Blend honey or Equal with buttermilk. Stir into mixture.

4. Cover and refrigerate for at least 1 hour before serving, stirring once or twice.

YIELD: 5 servings (1 cup each)

NOTES:
1. Flavor will be pointedly sweeter with Equal.
2. Zucchini, generally prepared with skin, is peeled here to reduce bitterness.

	CALORIES	SODIUM
Per serving:	87	50
With dried tarragon	No appreciable difference	
With Equal	75	50

Red Cabbage Slaw (15 minutes)

Use food processor

1   ¾-pound head crisp red cabbage (you will need 4 cups shredded cabbage)
1   small carrot, scrubbed
1   small onion, peeled
1   large tart apple, peeled and cored
⅓   cup loosely packed parsley flowerets, washed and well dried
1   teaspoon dried tarragon leaves, crumbled

1   teaspoon prepared Dijon mustard (no salt added)
3   tablespoons apple juice (no sugar added)
1   tablespoon each fresh lemon juice and tarragon vinegar
¾   cup low-fat plain yogurt

1. Fit food processor with shredding disc. Shred first 3 ingredients. Transfer to bowl. Fit processor with steel blade. Process apple and parsley until chopped. Combine with cabbage. Sprinkle with tarragon leaves. Toss.

2. In another bowl, combine mustard, apple juice, lemon juice, and tarragon vinegar; whisk to blend. Pour over cabbage mixture and toss. Stir in yogurt.

3. Cover and let mixture marinate in refrigerator for at least 1 hour before serving, stirring from time to time.

YIELD: Serves 5

	CALORIES	SODIUM
Per serving:	92.5	56

Yam Salad (15 minutes)

Use nonstick skillet

2 yams (1 pound), peeled
1 tablespoon tarragon vinegar
2 tablespoons apple juice (no sugar added)
2 teaspoons sweet unsalted margarine-butter blend (page 182) or sweet unsalted corn oil margarine

3 tablespoons coarsely chopped shallots
1 teaspoon Herb 'n Spice Mix (page 177)
2 tablespoons minced parsley or dill or a combination of both
3 tablespoons low-fat plain yogurt

1. Slice yams in food processor or by hand ¼-inch thick. (For quick hand slicing, cut each yam in half lengthwise. Lay cut side on board. Then proceed to slice.) Drop into saucepan of rapidly boiling water. Boil for 8 minutes. Drain. Transfer to bowl. Sprinkle with tarragon vinegar and apple juice. Place in freezer for 5 minutes to quick-cool.

2. Heat margarine-butter blend in nonstick skillet. Sauté shallots for 2 minutes, stirring often. Do not brown. Pour over cooled yams.

3. Sprinkle and stir mixture gently with slices. Then fold in parsley or dill and yogurt. Serve at room temperature or chilled.

YIELD: Serves 4

Per serving:
With margarine, dill

	CALORIES	SODIUM
	132.5	22.5
	No appreciable difference	

New Tomato-Mint Salad (15 minutes)

¼ cup raw bulgur
3 tablespoons fresh lemon juice
2 tablespoons wine vinegar (see Note)
1 tablespoon olive oil (see Note)
½ teaspoon dried tarragon leaves, crushed
4 dashes ground red (cayenne) pepper

1 pound ripe thin-skinned tomatoes, coarsely chopped
1 small sweet red onion, peeled and thinly sliced
2 small scallions, coarsely chopped
½ cup loosely packed fresh mint, chopped
2 tablespoons minced parsley

1. Wash bulgur through strainer. Transfer to bowl. Cover with cold water and let stand for 30 minutes. Drain in strainer, pressing with spoon to fully drain out water.

2. While bulgur is soaking, prepare dressing. Combine lemon juice with wine vinegar, oil, tarragon, and ground red pepper. Beat to blend with fork.

3. Place tomatoes, onion, scallions, mint, and parsley in bowl. Toss gently. Add drained bulgur. Pour dressing over mixture, tossing very gently.

YIELD: Serves 4

NOTE: The success of this simple salad depends upon fresh mint and the quality of the vinegar and oil. Pure wine vinegar aged in wood (6 percent acidity) is magnificent. Cold pressed extra virgin olive oil (you'll notice how little is used here) gives lots of flavor for little calories. Both products are imported but available in most supermarkets.

	CALORIES	SODIUM
Per serving:	113	13

Salad Dressings

Fastest Recipes

Lively and Light Salad Dressing (10 minutes)

⅓ cup each tomato juice (no salt added) and tarragon vinegar
¼ cup Italian olive oil or peanut oil
1 tablespoon minced dried onions
2 teaspoons Herb 'n Spice Mix (page 177)
½ teaspoon dried mustard
1 tablespoon minced parsley

1. Combine all ingredients in jar and shake well.

2. Let stand for 10 minutes. Shake again, and serve.

YIELD: About ¾ cup

VARIATION: Add ½ teaspoon each curry powder (no salt added) and tomato paste (no salt added) before shaking.

NOTE: This dressing will stay fresh for 2 or 3 days in tightly closed jar, well refrigerated.

	CALORIES	SODIUM
Per tablespoon:	45	3
With peanut oil	No appreciable difference	
Variation	No appreciable difference	

Zesty Salad Dressing (10 minutes)

⅓ cup each tomato puree (no salt added) and Delicious Chicken Stock (page 162)
2 teaspoons minced dried onions
1½ teaspoons Herb 'n Spice Mix (page 177)
1 teaspoon tarragon or wine vinegar

2 teaspoons arrowroot flour
1 egg yolk
1 teaspoon prepared Dijon mustard (no salt added)
4 teaspoons fresh lemon juice
¼ cup Italian olive oil

1. In saucepan, combine first 4 listed ingredients. Heat to simmering point. Whisk in arrowroot flour. Let cool.

2. In small bowl, combine and whisk egg yolk, mustard, and lemon juice until well blended. Then slowly dribble in oil while whisking. Mixture will be very thick.

3. Whisk in cooled stock mixture. Transfer to jar and chill.

YIELD: About ¾ cup

NOTES:

1. Salad dressing will thin down slightly after addition of stock mixture, but will thicken when chilled.

2. Mixture may be prepared with food blender. Here's how: Complete step 1. Assemble all ingredients in step 2 in food blender. Blend for 1 minute on high speed. Then, with machine on, dribble in oil. When all oil is absorbed, slowly add stock mixture.

	CALORIES	SODIUM
Per tablespoon:	53	5

Fruit Salad Dressing (10 minutes)

3   tablespoons each apple juice and pineapple juice (no sugar added), and fresh orange juice
1   teaspoon prepared Dijon mustard (no salt added)
1   tablespoon each wine vinegar and fresh lemon juice

½   teaspoon Indian Spice Mix (page 178)
2   tablespoons Italian olive oil
2   tablespoons minced parsley

1. Combine all ingredients in jar and shake well.

2. Let stand for 10 minutes. Shake again before serving.

YIELD: About ⅔ cup

NOTE: This salad dressing tastes best if prepared and used same day.

	CALORIES	SODIUM
Per tablespoon:	29.5	1

Orange Salad Dressing (10 minutes)

Use food blender

2   tablespoons Italian olive oil
⅓   cup tarragon vinegar or apple cider vinegar
2   tablespoons apple juice (no sugar added)
3   tablespoons frozen orange juice concentrate (no sugar added)

½   teaspoon prepared Dijon mustard (no salt added)
1½   teaspoons Barbeque Spice Mix (page 178)
2   tablespoons minced parsley

1. Combine all ingredients in food blender. Blend on high speed for 30 seconds.

2. Let stand for 5 minutes. Blend again for 5 seconds.

YIELD: ⅔ cup

NOTE: This salad dressing tastes best if prepared and used same day.

	CALORIES	SODIUM
Per tablespoon:	43	2.5
With apple cider vinegar		No appreciable difference

Mint Salad Dressing (10 minutes)

3 tablespoons each tarragon and wine vinegar
¼ cup each Italian olive oil and Delicious Chicken Stock (page 162)
½ teaspoon dried mustard

1 teaspoon dried minced onions
1 teaspoon each dried savory leaves, crushed, and dried mint, crumbled
4 dashes ground red (cayenne) pepper

1. Combine all ingredients in jar and shake well.

2. Let stand for 10 minutes. Shake again and serve.

YIELD: About ¾ cup

NOTE: This salad dressing will stay fresh for 1 or 2 days in tightly closed jar, well refrigerated.

	CALORIES	SODIUM
Per serving:	43	3.5

Desserts

Fastest Recipes

Spiced Sautéed Bananas with Pine Nuts (10 minutes)

Sweet and piquant, soft and crunchy, fruity and nutty, this dessert of exquisite contrasts is something to cheer about. Add this reason for one more hurrah: You can make it from start to finish in just 4 minutes.

Use nonstick skillet

2 teaspoons sweet unsalted corn oil margarine or sweet unsalted margarine-butter blend (page 182)
2 small ripe bananas, sliced

1 tablespoon pine nuts
½ teaspoon each ground cinnamon and ginger
1 teaspoon fresh lemon juice

1. Melt margarine in nonstick skillet over medium-high heat, spreading across skillet with spatula. Add bananas, spreading out into one layer. Strew pine nuts around banana slices.

Sprinkle with spices. Sauté for 1½ minutes. Turn gently with spatula. Sauté for 1½ minutes.

2. Sprinkle with lemon juice. Stir, and serve.

YIELD: Serves 2

NOTE: There is a variety of ginger called Jamaica ginger which is sharp tasting and particularly delicious in this dessert.

	CALORIES	SODIUM
Per serving:	143	2.5
With margarine-butter blend	No appreciable difference	

Baked Stuffed Pears (10 minutes)

These full-bodied pears, stuffed with raisins and date sugar, then mantled with a sweet mulled wine sauce, satisfy your dessert-craving with style.

Preheat oven to 425°F

3   tablespoons raisins
2   tablespoons date sugar (page 182)
1   tablespoon plus ¼ cup Marsala wine
2   large firm, ripe d'Anjou pears, peeled and cored, left whole

1   tablespoon each fresh lemon juice and frozen orange juice concentrate (no sugar added)
½   teaspoon each ground coriander and cinnamon

1. In cup, combine raisins, date sugar, and 1 tablespoon Marsala wine.
2. Stand pears in upright position in 1¾-quart baking casserole. Fill cored cavities with equal amounts of raisin mixture, pushing down gently with finger.
3. Heat ¼ cup Marsala, lemon juice, orange juice concentrate, and spices to simmering point. Spoon over pears evenly.

4. Bake, uncovered, in a preheated oven 35 to 40 minutes (cooking time will depend upon ripeness of pears), basting with sauce 3 times at equal intervals, and again when done. Sauce and pears will be a rich cinnamon brown. Cut each pear in half. Serve warm or at room temperature.

YIELD: Serves 4

Per serving:

	CALORIES	SODIUM
	123.5	5.5

Fresh Figs with Apricot-Strawberry Sauce

(10 minutes)

Here ripe figs, lustily sweet, are embraced by a fruit sauce with just the right counterpoints of sharpness to create a deliciously chic confiture.

Use food blender

¼   cup part-skim ricotta cheese
1   16-ounce can drained apricot halves, packed in water (no sugar added)
¼   teaspoon each ground coriander and cinnamon

5   teaspoons unsweetened strawberry conserves (page 182)
4   large fresh figs, sliced
    Fresh mint leaves

1. Combine first 3 ingredients and 3 teaspoons strawberry conserves in food blender. Blend on high speed until smooth. There will be ¾ cup.

2. Arrange sliced figs on 4 flat salad-size dishes (1 fig per serving), overlapping slices. Spoon sauce around fig slices. Top each serving with ½ teaspoon conserves. Garnish with mint leaves, and serve.

YIELD: Serves 4

	CALORIES	SODIUM
Per serving:	94	5

Kiwi, Fresh Dates, and Grand Marnier with Peanut Butter—Pineapple Topping (10 minutes)

Who can ask for anything more?

5 fresh dates, pitted and sliced
2 ripe kiwi fruit, peeled and sliced
1 tablespoon Grand Marnier liqueur

2 tablespoons Peanut Butter—Pineapple Topping (page 161)

1. Combine sliced fruit in bowl. Sprinkle with liqueur, stirring to combine. Let stand for 5 minutes.

2. Serve in 2 decorative dessert dishes. Top each dessert with 1 tablespoon Peanut Butter—Pineapple Topping.

YIELD: 2 servings

	CALORIES	SODIUM
Per serving:	159	12.5

Ethereal Apricot Cream (10 minutes)

A light and engaging bittersweet confection with a cloudlike consistency. When chilled and set, it can also be enjoyed as a heavenly chiffonlike dessert, or as a filling for your pie in the sky.

Use electric mixer

⅔ cup evaporated milk
1 cup chilled unsweetened Festive Breakfast Apricots (page 114), chopped
¼ cup part-skim ricotta cheese

⅔ cup (6 ounces) pineapple juice (no sugar added)
1 envelope plain gelatin
1 teaspoon finely grated orange rind

1. Pour evaporated milk into large mixing bowl. Place bowl and whipping utensils in freezer, positioning bowl in direct contact with metal in freezer compartment. Chill until mixture freezes.

2. While milk is chilling, whisk apricots and ricotta cheese in large bowl until well blended.

3. Pour pineapple juice into small saucepan. Sprinkle with gelatin. Let soften for 2 minutes. Add orange rind and heat (do not boil) until gelatin dissolves, stirring constantly. Whisk into apricot mixture. Chill until it begins to thicken.

4. Whip frozen milk until stiff. Whisk one-third into thickened apricot mixture. Fold in balance.

5. Spoon into 6 decorative dessert dishes. Serve at once (mixture will be soft and creamy); or chill until set (mixture will be chiffonlike in texture).

YIELD: Serves 6

VARATIONS:

1. Serve as a pie. Prepare the easiest-ever no-bake pie base from Peanut Butter—Pineapple Chiffon Pudding Pie (page 151), following directions in step 1. Complete step 4 in this recipe and spoon apricot mixture into prepared base. Chill until firm, allowing at least 2 hours to set. Cut with cold moistened knife. Pie will serve 6.

2. If you prefer your desserts very sweet (I don't), add 1 tablespoon honey or a 1-gram packet of Equal in step 3.

	CALORIES	SODIUM
Per serving:	114.5	40
As a pie, per serving:	134	40.5
With honey, add	+6	+.5
With Equal	No appreciable difference	

Spiced-Grape Applesauce (10 minutes)

Grape juice, two sweet spices (nutmeg and cinnamon), and one that's bittersweet (coriander) place this applesauce in a class by itself. Cook a double recipe, and employ the surplus as foundations for the two elegant confections that follow. One is a festive Apple Whip (with an even more festive frozen custard-y variation), and the other is my light-as-air Apple Cream Pouf.

Use food mill or strainer

1½ pounds Cortland or McIntosh apples, or a mixture of both, cored and sliced

½ cup grape juice (no sugar added)

½ teaspoon each ground coriander, cinnamon, and freshly grated nutmeg

1 teaspoon fresh lemon juice

1 1-gram packet Equal (optional)

1. Combine all ingredients except Equal in heavy-bottomed saucepan. Bring to a boil. Reduce heat to simmering. Cover and simmer for 10 minutes, stirring several times during first 5 minutes. Uncover. Let cool for 5 minutes.

2. Pour into food mill and puree. Taste. Stir in Equal, if desired. Serve warm or chilled.

YIELD: Serves 5

	CALORIES	SODIUM
Per serving:	92	2
With Equal	No appreciable difference	

Festive Apple Whip (10 minutes)

Use electric mixer

½ cup evaporated milk
1 cup Spiced-Grape Applesauce (page 141)

1 teaspoon pure vanilla extract

1. Pour evaporated milk into large mixing bowl. Place bowl and whipping utensils in freezer, positioning bowl in direct contact with metal. Chill until mixture freezes. Whip until stiff.

2. In another bowl, whisk cheese with applesauce and liqueur until smooth.

3. Fold in whipped milk. Serve immediately.

YIELD: Serves 4

VARIATION: For a frozen custard consistency, complete steps 1 and 2. Place in freezer for about 2 hours. Whisk or beat vigorously. Serve immediately.

	CALORIES	SODIUM
Per serving:	103.5	38.5

Apple Cream Pouf (10 minutes)

Use electric mixer

⅓ cup evaporated milk
¼ cup part-skim ricotta cheese
1 cup Spiced-Grape Applesauce (page 141)

1 tablespoon Amaretto, Grand Marnier, or any distinctively flavored liqueur

1. Pour evaporated milk into large mixing bowl. Place bowl and whipping utensils in freezer, positioning bowl in direct contact with metal. Chill until milk freezes, then whip on high speed until stiff.

2. Place applesauce in large bowl. Stir in vanilla. Whisk in one-third of whipped milk. Then fold in balance with wooden spoon.

3. Pile into decorative dessert dishes, and serve immediately.

YIELD: Serves 4

	CALORIES	SODIUM
Per serving:	115.5	31.5
With Grand Marnier	No appreciable difference	

Apricot Tea Loaf (10 minutes)

This is a hearty sweet—not quite a cake, not quite a bread—that exudes healthfulness and the joy of life. Enjoy its bracing qualities at teatime or anytime.

Preheat oven to 350°F

¾ cup each unbleached flour and stone-ground whole-wheat flour
2 teaspoons baking powder
¼ cup The Healthy Sweetener (page 182)
3 tablespoons peanut oil
2 tablespoons honey
2 eggs (use 1 yolk, 2 whites)

½ cup chilled unsweetened Festive Breakfast Apricots (page 114), chopped
⅓ cup low-fat plain yogurt
¼ teaspoon sweet unsalted margarine-butter blend (page 182) or sweet unsalted corn oil margarine for pan

1. Sift flours and baking powder into large mixing bowl. Stir in The Healthy Sweetener.

2. In another bowl, whisk oil with honey until blended. Then whisk in eggs. Stir into dry ingredients rapidly.

3. Combine apricots with yogurt. Fold into batter.

4. Spoon into small shortening-greased loaf pan (7⅜″ × 3⅝″ × 2¼″). Bake in center section of preheated oven for 45 to 50 minutes. Finished cake should be browned and toothpick inserted into center of cake should come out clean. Place pan on rack and let cool for 5 minutes. Remove loaf from pan. Let cool on rack before slicing.

YIELD: 12 or 14 slices

NOTE: Wonderful served warm the next day.

	CALORIES	SODIUM
12 slices, per slice:	107.5	58
14 slices, per slice:	92	50
With margarine	No appreciable difference	

My Fruit Zabaione (10 minutes)

When my husband is asked to name the three greatest desserts of the world, he answers, "Three zabaiones." My healthful version of this nonpareil custard (no egg yolks, no sugar) retains the soft velvety smoothness of the original, and the just-right proportion of dreamy Marsala, but has its own fruited and spiced elegance. And now for the unexpected: rush to the variation—zabaione frozen custard or ice cream.

Use electric mixer

⅔ cup chilled evaporated milk
3 ounces partially thawed orange juice concentrate (no sugar added)
4 ounces partially thawed apple juice concentrate (no sugar added)
½ teaspoon grated orange rind (preferably from navel orange)

2 tablespoons sweet Marsala wine (optional)
2 dashes ground clove, or 1 whole clove, crushed
¼ teaspoon ground cinnamon

1. Pour evaporated milk into large mixing bowl. Place bowl and whipping utensils in freezer, positioning bowl in direct contact with metal. Chill until mixture freezes (about 30 minutes). Whip on high speed until stiff.

2. Combine juice concentrates, orange rind, wine, and spices in large bowl. Whisk until blended. Using whisk, gently fold whipped milk into concentrate mixture until all concentrate is absorbed.

3. Pile into decorative dessert dishes. Serve immediately.

YIELD: Serves 6

VARIATION: Complete recipe through step 2. Then transfer mixture into freezer tray which has been rinsed in cold water. Place in center section of your freezer (bottom of tray *should not be* in contact with metal). Freeze for 2 to 3 hours for frozen custard consistency, and for 4 to 5 hours for the consistency of ice cream. Freezing time may vary slightly with width and depth of freezer tray and efficiency of freezer.

	CALORIES	SODIUM
Per serving, zabaione or ice cream:	108.5	34
With Marsala	116	34

10-Minute Spice Cake (10 minutes)

As a cake or as a muffin (see Variation 1), this warmhearted sweet is just right for cozy breakfasts when frost limns the windowpanes. Or for anytime when a wonderful inner glow is your heart's desire.

Use electric mixer

Preheat oven to 350°F

1½ cups unbleached flour
1½ teaspoons baking powder
1 teaspoon each ground ginger and coriander
½ teaspoon ground cinnamon
¼ cup sweet unsalted margarine-butter blend (page 182), plus ¼ teaspoon for pan

¼ cup date sugar (page 182)
1 teaspoon pure vanilla extract
2 eggs
⅓ cup each buttermilk (no salt added) and pineapple juice (no sugar added), combined

1. Sift flour, baking powder, and spices into bowl. Set aside.

2. In large bowl of mixing machine, combine ¼ cup margarine-butter blend, date sugar, and vanilla. Beat on medium-high speed until well blended (about 1 minute). Add eggs. Beat on low speed for 30 seconds; then on high speed for 30 seconds.

3. On low speed, add dry ingredients alternately with buttermilk-pineapple mixture. Then beat on medium-high speed for 10 seconds.

4. Spoon into lightly greased small loaf pan (7⅜" × 3⅝" × 2¼"). Bake in center section of preheated oven for 50 to 55 minutes. Finished loaf should be brown all over and toothpick inserted in center should come out clean. Place pan on rack for 5 minutes. Loosen cake with blunt knife. Remove from pan and let cool completely for even slicing.

YIELD: 14 slices (½ inch each)

NOTE: Use this cake as a base for my Spiced Apple Cake (page 149).

VARIATIONS:

1. Prepare 12 small muffins. Lightly grease muffin cups with ½ teaspoon margarine-butter blend. Three-quarter fill with batter. Bake 15 to 18 minutes, or until delicately browned and muffins recede from sides of pan.

2. A blended combination of 3 tablespoons low-fat plain yogurt and 2 tablespoons nonfat liquid milk may be substituted for buttermilk.

	CALORIES	SODIUM
Per slice:	100.5	41
Per muffin:	112.5	47
Variation 2	No appreciable difference	

Two New Milk Shakes

The reason you've never tasted anything like them before is: One is based on a fruit sauce, and the other on a nut butter-fruit topping, and both bases appear in this book for the first time. For milk-shake lovers with a passion for the unusual.

Pink 'n Pretty Milk Shake (10 minutes)

Use food blender

3 just-crushed ice cubes
½ cup nonfat liquid milk
¼ cup evaporated skim milk

3 tablespoons Roseate Fruit Sauce (page 155)

Place all ingredients in blender in order in which they're listed. Blend on high speed for 1 minute. Serve immediately.

YIELD: Serves 2

	CALORIES	SODIUM
Per serving:	78	66
With Roseate Fruit Sauce made with Equal	66	66

Thick 'n Satisfying Milk Shake (10 minutes)

Use food blender

3 just-crushed ice cubes
½ cup nonfat liquid milk
2 tablespoons Peanut Butter—Pineapple Topping (page 161)

1 1-gram packet Equal, or 1 teaspoon honey

Place all ingredients in blender in order in which they're listed. Blend on high speed for 1 minute. Serve immediately.

YIELD: Serves 2

NOTE: Mixture prepared with honey will be thick and drinkable. Mixture prepared with Equal will be extra-thick and spoonable.

	CALORIES	SODIUM
Per serving:	86.5	35
With honey	95	35

Faster Recipes

Strawberry Mousse (15 minutes)

Definition of a mousse: a froth—light, airy, smooth, pretty, graceful, delicate, and, when it is prepared to perfection, irresistible. Example: this dessert.

Use food blender

Use electric mixer (optional)

1½ cups hulled and sliced fresh strawberries (about 1½ pints)

½ cup each grape and apple juice
(no sugar added)

1 tablespoon fresh lemon juice

¼ cup part-skim ricotta cheese

1 package unflavored gelatin

2 1-gram packets Equal

2 tablespoons Calvados or Grand
Marnier

2 egg whites, stiffly beaten

1. Reserve 12 slices fresh strawberries for garnish. In small heavy-bottomed saucepan, combine balance of strawberries, grape juice, apple juice, and lemon juice. Cover and bring to simmering point and simmer for 2 minutes. Let cool for 2 minutes.

2. With slotted spoon, transfer strawberries and ¼ cup cooking liquid to food blender. Add ricotta cheese. Blend until smooth. Pour into bowl.

3. Sprinkle gelatin into remaining cooking liquid, stirring to dissolve. Add to pureed mixture. Stir in Equal and liqueur. Chill until mixture begins to thicken (about 20 minutes).

4. Whisk in one third beaten egg whites. Fold in balance.

5. Spoon into 6 decorative dessert dishes. Garnish each dessert with 2 slices reserved strawberries. Chill until set.

YIELD: Serves 6

VARIATION: One tablespoon honey may be substituted for Equal.

	CALORIES	SODIUM
Per serving:	73	13
With Grand Marnier	No appreciable difference	
With honey	82.5	13

Party Fresh-Fruit Bouquets (15 minutes)

A succulent sweet mélange of fresh fruit and their juices enlivened by just the right touch of a cognac flavored with orange peel.

1 cup each diced fresh pineapple, honeydew balls, sliced mango, and diced seeded watermelon
1 tablespoon date sugar (page 182) (optional)

2 tablespoons fresh orange juice
2 tablespoons Grand Marnier liqueur
¼ teaspoon each ground coriander and freshly grated nutmeg

1. Place pineapple and its exuded juices in large bowl with honeydew, mango, and watermelon. Sprinkle with date sugar.
2. Combine orange juice with Grand Marnier and spices. Pour over fruit. Gently toss.
3. Serve immediately in decorative bowl or in hollowed-out melon or pineapple halves.

YIELD: Serves 6

VARIATION: Totally refreshing salad served on crisp lettuce leaves with 2 tablespoons each per portion of part-skim ricotta cheese spooned atop mixture.

YIELD: Serves 8

	CALORIES	SODIUM
Per serving:	69.5	6.5
With lettuce and ricotta	113.5	13.5

Fast Recipes

Pretty Pink Strawberry Sorbet (20 minutes)

A rich-tasting, fruity, supernally sweet confection for a blissful ending to any meal. Taste titillations: those soupçons of orange rind, almond essence, and nutmeg.

Use food blender

Use electric mixer (optional)

1 8-ounce can chilled pineapple chunks packed in unsweetened pineapple juice
1 pint fresh strawberries, washed, hulled, and sliced
2 tablespoons fresh lemon juice
1½ teaspoons plain gelatin

⅔ cup chilled evaporated skim milk
4 1-gram packets Equal
¼ teaspoon freshly grated nutmeg
1 tablespoon sweet Marsala wine (optional)
2 egg whites, stiffly beaten

1. Drain juice from pineapples. Place pineapples in food blender and juice in small heavy-bottomed saucepan. To saucepan add strawberries and lemon juice. Bring to simmering point. Reduce heat. Cover and simmer for 3 minutes. Stir in gelatin. Continue stirring until dissolved. Let cool.

2. To blender add evaporated skim milk, Equal, and nutmeg. Blend on high speed until smooth and creamy textured. Pour into bowl.

3. Pour cooled strawberries into blender. Blend for 30 seconds. Add to milk mixture. Stir in Marsala.

4. Turn into freezer tray that has been rinsed in cold water. Place tray directly onto metal in freezer compartment of refrigerator. Freeze until mushy (1¼ to 1½ hours). Turn into bowl. Whisk or beat until smooth.

5. Using whisk, gently fold and whisk in beaten egg whites. Pour mixture back into freezer tray. This time do not place tray in direct contact with metal. Freeze for 2 to 3 hours or until firm but not hard. Serve in decorative dessert dishes (champagne glasses would be superb).

YIELD: Serves 6

	CALORIES	SODIUM
Per serving:	82	50.5
With Marsala	86	50.5

Spiced Apple Cake (20 minutes)

This is a gorgeous cake to gaze upon—a pastry-cart, a window-display kind of cake. And it's just as wonderful to taste.

Use electric mixer
Preheat oven to 350°F

1 lemon
  Grated rind of ½ lemon
3 Golden Delicious apples
1 tablespoon date sugar (page 182)
1 teaspoon sweet unsalted margarine-butter blend (page 182) plus ¼ teaspoon for pan
½ teaspoon ground cinnamon

2 tablespoons chopped walnuts
1 recipe 10-Minute Spice Cake (page 145)
1 tablespoon raisins
2 1-gram packets Equal
1 tablespoon unsweetened pineapple juice

1. Prepare apple topping first. Squeeze juice of lemon into large bowl. Add grated rind. Core, pare, quarter, and cut apples into ⅜-inch slices. Drop into lemon juice mixture as apples are sliced, stirring to coat. Set aside.

2. In another bowl, combine and blend date sugar, 1 teaspoon margarine-butter blend, cinnamon, and walnuts. Set aside.

3. Prepare 10-Minute Spice Cake. Lightly grease a 9-inch-square baking

pan with margarine-butter blend. Evenly spread batter into pan, making certain that corners are filled. Arrange 4 rows of apple slices fairly close to each other on top of batter, laying slices on their sides. Pour any lemon juice residue left in bowl over apples.

4. Sprinkle evenly with date sugar mixture and then with raisins. Lightly press entire topping into batter. Bake

in center section of preheated oven for 55 to 60 minutes. Cake is fully baked when batter comes away from sides of pan and is lightly browned.

5. Place pan on rack. Dissolve Equal in pineapple juice. Sprinkle evenly over cake. Let cook for at least 30 minutes before cutting into 12 squares. Serve warm or at room temperature.

YIELD: 12 squares

NOTE: Squares freeze beautifully if wrapped individually in aluminum foil. Reheat in preheated 350°F oven. Serve warm.

	CALORIES	SODIUM
Per square:	159	47.5

Crisp and Chewy Oatmeal Cookies (20 minutes)

Add "subtly spiced and buttermilked," and you have the whole picture.

Use electric mixer

Preheat oven to 375°F

½ cup old-fashioned rolled oats
¾ cup buttermilk (no salt added)
¼ cup raisins
1⅔ cups unbleached flour
2 teaspoons baking powder
½ teaspoon ground cardamom
¾ teaspoon ground cinnamon
⅓ cup The Healthy Sweetener (page 182)

2 tablespoons each peanut oil and sweet unsalted margarine-butter blend (page 182) or sweet unsalted corn oil margarine, plus ½ teaspoon for pan
2 tablespoons honey
1 egg
1 teaspoon pure vanilla extract

1. Combine rolled oats, buttermilk, and raisins in small bowl, stirring to blend.

2. Sift flour, baking powder, and spices into another bowl. Crumble The Healthy Sweetener with fingers and stir into flour mixture.

3. In mixing bowl, beat the oil and 2 tablespoons margarine-butter blend

with honey on medium speed of mixing machine until smooth. Add egg and vanilla and beat until well blended.

4. Add buttermilk mixture alternately with flour mixture, beating on medium speed, until both mixtures are incorporated.

5. Lightly grease 2 cookie sheets

(11½″ × 15½″) with remaining ½ teaspoon margarine-butter blend. Drop cookies by spoonfuls onto sheets, arranging 16 cookies per sheet. Then flatten each cookie with moistened fork to ¼-inch thickness.

6. Bake for 10 minutes in center section of preheated oven. Then turn heat up to 400°F and bake 8 to 10 minutes, or until cookies are lightly browned on top and crispy on the bottom and around the edges. For best flavor, cool cookies completely on rack before serving.

YIELD: 32 cookies

VARIATION: Add 1 teaspoon finely grated orange rind in Step 4.

	CALORIES	SODIUM
Per cookie:	58	21.5
With margarine, orange rind		No appreciable difference

Peanut Butter—Pineapple Chiffon Pie

(20 minutes)

If you're frantically flipping the pages of this book to find the richest-tasting dessert, stop here.

Use electric mixer

1 teaspoon sweet unsalted margarine-butter blend (page 182) or sweet unsalted corn oil margarine, melted
3 tablespoons each toasted wheat germ (no sugar added), date sugar, and The Healthy Sweetener (page 182), combined
1 recipe Peanut Butter—Pineapple Topping (page 161)
¼ cup water

1 envelope plus 1 teaspoon plain gelatin
4 teaspoons frozen orange juice concentrate (no sugar added)
1 cup nonfat liquid milk
¼ teaspoon freshly grated nutmeg
2 teaspoons finely grated orange rind
½ teaspoon almond extract
2 egg whites, stiffly beaten
1 orange slice

1. With pastry brush, spread margarine-butter blend across and around sides of 6- or 8-inch pie plate. Sprinkle with wheat germ, date sugar, and The Healthy Sweetener, pressing against dish to hold. Refrigerate until ready to fill.

2. Place Peanut Butter—Pineapple Topping in large bowl. Set aside.

3. Pour water into saucepan. Sprinkle with gelatin. Let soften for 3 minutes. Then heat and stir until dissolved. Stir in orange juice concentrate and milk. Pour into bowl with topping. Whisk until smooth.

4. Whisk in nutmeg, half of orange rind, and almond extract. Place in freezer compartment of refrigerator

or in ice bath to chill until thickened (about 20 minutes).

5. Whisk in one-third beaten egg whites. Fold in balance.

6. Spoon into prepared pie plate.

Sprinkle with balance of orange rind. Cut orange slice into 4 pieces and arrange a star in center of pie. Chill until set (about 2 hours), and cut with cold moistened knife.

YIELD: Serves 8

NOTES:

1. Mixture will thicken rapidly in step 4 if topping (third listed ingredient) is chilled.

2. Add 1 tablespoon Grand Marnier liqueur in step 4 and eliminate almond extract.

	CALORIES	SODIUM
Per serving:	187.5	38.5
With margarine	No appreciable difference	
With Grand Marnier	No appreciable difference	

Sauces, Marinades, Toppings, and a Stock

They have one thing in common: They elevate the joy of foods.

My stock—the aromatic commingled essences of chicken, herbs, spices, and vegetables—invigorates sauces, soups, and gravies. My sauces—either wine, or chicken, or mushroom, or tomato, or fruit flavored—glorify appropriate meats, fish, fowl, pasta, vegetables, and desserts. My toppings—one, light, airy, and citrusy; the other, creamy and tangy with yogurt—brighten salads and sweets. And my marinades—

But they deserve a paragraph all their own.

My marinades are among my proudest creations. They are consummately novel combinations of fruit juices, vinegars, wines, and oils seasoned with a diversity of flavorings. I regard them as my magic potions—for they transmute toughness to tenderness and the ordinary to the zesty, the piquant, the smart, the toothsome, the savory, the pungent—the irresistible. And yet they're simple to make, do their job while you're free to enjoy your leisure; and they're so, so easy on the purse. (Why don't you try a little magic of your own by altering proportions and ingredients? Inventing new taste thrills is a great thrill.)

Sauces

Fastest Recipes

Delicate Wine Sauce (10 minutes)

¼ cup minced shallots
¼ cup tarragon vinegar
½ cup each dry red wine and Delicious Chicken Stock (page 162)
½ teaspoon dried tarragon leaves, crumbled
1 tablespoon Ready Duxelles (page 180), or 2 large fresh mushrooms, washed, dried, trimmed, and minced

2 tablespoons minced watercress leaves
2 tablespoons arrowroot flour dissolved in 2 teaspoons water
2 dashes ground red (cayenne) pepper

1. In small heavy-bottomed enameled saucepan, cook shallots with vinegar over medium heat, uncovered, until all liquid is reduced (about 3 minutes).

2. Add wine, stock, and tarragon. Simmer uncovered for 4 minutes. Strain into bowl, pressing out juices.

3. Pour strained sauce back into saucepan. Add duxelles or fresh mushrooms and watercress. Simmer for 2 minutes.

4. Dribble in arrowroot mixture while stirring. Stir in ground red pepper. Mixture will be lightly thickened. Serve very hot in sauceboat with beef, lamb, or pork.

YIELD: Scant cup

VARIATION: Remove saucepan from heat at end of step 4. For a creamier taste, stir in 2 tablespoons evaporated skim milk. Serve immediately.

	CALORIES	SODIUM
Per tablespoon:	8.5	6.5
With mushrooms	No appreciable difference	
With variation	10	9

Creamy Chicken Sauce (10 minutes)

1¼ cups Delicious Chicken Stock (page 162)
¼ cup medium-dry sherry
1½ teaspoons tomato paste (no salt added)
½ teaspoon each dried tarragon leaves, crumbled, and chili con carne seasoning (no salt or pepper added)

1 teaspoon dehydrated onion flakes, broken up
1 tablespoon minced parsley
1 tablespoon arrowroot flour dissolved in 1 tablespoon water
3 tablespoons evaporated skim milk
3 dashes ground red (cayenne) pepper

1. In small, heavy-bottomed enameled saucepan, combine stock and sherry. Bring to simmering point. Simmer, uncovered, for 2 minutes.

2. Whisk in tomato paste, tarragon, chili con carne seasoning, onion flakes, and parsley.

3. While whisking, dribble in arrowroot mixture. Sauce will thicken to consistency of sour cream.

4. Remove from heat. Stir in evaporated skim milk and ground red pepper. Serve immediately.

YIELD: About 1¼ cups

	CALORIES	SODIUM
Per tablespoon:	7	9.5

Roseate Fruit Sauce (10 minutes)

Use food blender

12 canned pineapple chunks, packed in pineapple juice (no sugar added), drained
3 tablespoons pineapple juice (no sugar added)
1 pint ripe fresh strawberries, hulled, rinsed and sliced

2 tablespoons sweet Marsala wine
¼ teaspoon ground coriander
1 teaspoon arrowroot flour
2 tablespoons honey, or 1 packet Equal (1 gram)

1. Place pineapple, 2 tablespoons pineapple juice, strawberries, wine, and coriander in heavy-bottomed saucepan. Bring to boil. Reduce heat to simmering. Cover and cook for 3 minutes. Uncover.

2. Dissolve arrowroot flour in remaining tablespoon pineapple juice. Stir into mixture. Let cool for 5 minutes.

3. Pour into blender and puree until smooth. Stir in honey or Equal. Serve chilled.

YIELD: About 1 cup

VARIATIONS:

The following suggestions are for one serving.

1. Spoon 3 tablespoons sauce over ⅓ cup chilled cooked rice.

2. Peel and split a small banana. Spread with 2 tablespoons part-skim ricotta cheese. Top with 2 tablespoons sauce.

3. Spoon 2 tablespoons sauce over slices of 10-Minute Spice Cake (page 145).

4. Serve in sauceboat with Banana Hotcake (page 115). Allow 21.5 calories per tablespoon with honey and 13.5 calories per tablespoon with Equal.

5. Use in Pink 'n Pretty Milk Shake (page 146).

	CALORIES	SODIUM
Per tablespoon:	21.5	.5
With Equal	13.5	.5
With chilled cooked rice	116	1
With chilled cooked rice and Equal	65	1
With bananas	168	2.5
With bananas and Equal	151.5	2.5
With 10-Minute Spice Cake	139	40.5
With 10-Minute Spice Cake and Equal	122.5	40.5
With hotcake only; add sauce to taste	83	49
With Pink 'n Pretty Milk Shake and Equal	66	66

Quick Mushroom Sauce (10 minutes)

½ pound snow-white fresh mushrooms, washed, dried, and coarsely chopped

¼ cup each Marsala wine and apple juice (no sugar added)

¾ cup Delicious Chicken Stock (page 162)

4 teaspoons minced dried onions

1 teaspoon Herb 'n Spice Mix (page 177)

2 tablespoons arrowroot flour

1 tablespoon minced parsley

3 tablespoons evaporated skim milk

2 dashes ground red (cayenne) pepper (optional)

1. In heavy-bottomed stainless-steel or enameled saucepan, combine mushrooms, wine, apple juice, stock, dried onions, and Herb 'n Spice Mix. Bring to a boil. Reduce heat to simmering. Cover and simmer for 10 minutes.

2. Uncover. Turn heat up to slow-boil. Whisk in arrowroot flour until blended. Add parsley. Simmer for 3 minutes.

3. Stir in evaporated skim milk and ground red pepper. Reheat, if necessary, to just under simmering point. Serve immediately.

YIELD: About 1½ cups

NOTE: The texture of sauce is best if prepared just before serving.

	CALORIES	SODIUM
Per tablespoon:	11	7.5
With ground red pepper	No appreciable difference	

Faster Recipe

Fresh Tomato Sauce with Mint (15 minutes)

Use food processor

Use iron skillet

1 medium onion, cut into 1-inch pieces
3 cloves garlic, halved
1 medium-size sweet green pepper, seeded, cut into 1-inch pieces
¼ cup each rinsed and well-dried mint leaves and parsley flowerets
1 tablespoon Italian olive oil
1 teaspoon curry powder (no salt added)

4 dashes ground red (cayenne) pepper
1 pound ripe egg tomatoes, cored and quartered
1 tablespoon tarragon vinegar
2 tablespoons tomato paste (no salt added)
¼ cup apple juice (no sugar added)

1. Fit food processor with steel blade. In work bowl combine onion, garlic, green pepper, mint, and parsley. Process on/off twice (mixture should be minced; do not over-process).

2. Heat oil in well-seasoned iron skillet until hot. Add mixture. Sprinkle with curry and ground red pepper. Sauté over medium-high heat until softened (about 4 minutes), stirring often.

3. While minced mixture is sautéing, place tomatoes in work bowl of food processor. Process on/off 4 times to coarsely chop tomatoes.

4. Sprinkle tarragon vinegar into skillet. Add chopped tomatoes and stir.

5. Combine tomato paste with apple juice, beating with fork to blend. Stir into skillet. Bring to simmering point. Reduce heat. Cover and simmer for 15 minutes, stirring once midway.

YIELD: Serves 4; 1½ cups

VARIATION: Cook 5 ounces Ronzoni Orzo (a rice-shaped pasta, no salt added) or spaghetti (no salt added) in rapidly boiling water for 12 minutes. Drain. Stir into finished sauce. Heat to simmering and serve.

	CALORIES	SODIUM
Per serving:	87	16
With pasta	139.5	16

Marinades

Fastest Recipes

Mixed Fruit Marinade (10 minutes)

1 teaspoon each ground ginger and dried rosemary leaves, crushed
⅓ cup grape juice (no sugar added)
2 tablespoons each apple juice (no sugar added) and fresh lemon juice

1 tablespoon each minced garlic and shallot
1 tablespoon minced parsley, or 1 teaspoon dried chervil leaves, crumbled

1. Combine all ingredients in a jar.

2. Shake well to blend.

YIELD: About ⅔ cup (enough to marinate a 3-pound chicken or roast)

	CALORIES	SODIUM
Per serving when dish serves 4: With chervil	23	3
	No appreciable difference	

Orange Marinade (10 minutes)

3 tablespoons wine vinegar
⅓ cup fresh orange juice
½ teaspoon each ground cinnamon, ginger, and dried savory leaves, crushed
4 dashes ground red (cayenne) pepper

1 tablespoon minced dried onions
1 tablespoon uncooked honey (see Note)
½ teaspoon aniseed, crushed

1. Combine all ingredients in a jar.

2. Shake well to blend.

YIELD: About ½ cup (enough to marinate a 3-pound chicken or roast)

NOTE: If you prefer not to use honey, include ½ teaspoon ground coriander.

	CALORIES	SODIUM
Per serving when dish serves 4:	36	5
Without honey, with coriander	20	4.5

Juniper Marinade (10 minutes)

1 tablespoon each frozen grapefruit
and orange concentrate (no sugar
added)
1 tablespoon Indian Spice Mix (page
178)
1 tablespoon juniper berries, well
crushed

2 teaspoons minced garlic
1/3 cup dry white wine
2 teaspoons finely grated orange
rind

1. Combine all ingredients in jar,
crushing frozen concentrate with
spoon until softened.

2. Shake to blend.

YIELD: About 3/4 cup (enough to marinate a 3-pound chicken or roast)

	CALORIES	SODIUM
Per serving when dish serves 4:	36	2

Barbeque Marinade I (10 minutes)

1 3/4 teaspoons Barbeque Spice Mix
(page 178)
1/3 cup Delicious Chicken Stock
(page 162)
3 tablespoons apple juice (no sugar
added)

2 teaspoons tomato paste (no salt
added)
1 tablespoon minced dried onions
1 tablespoon minced parsley

1. Combine all ingredients in a jar.
Shake well to blend.

2. Let stand for 3 minutes. Shake
again before using.

YIELD: About 1/2 cup (enough to marinate a 3-pound chicken or roast)

	CALORIES	SODIUM
Per serving when dish serves 4:	19	11.5

Barbeque Marinade II (10 minutes)

⅓ cup dry red wine
1½ teaspoons Barbeque Spice Mix (page 178)
1 teaspoon fresh lemon juice
¼ teaspoon grated lemon rind
2 teaspoons tomato paste (no salt added)

½ teaspoon dried chervil leaves, crumbled
2 teaspoons Italian olive oil
1 tablespoon minced shallots (optional)

1. Combine all ingredients in a jar.

2. Shake well to blend.

YIELD: About ½ cup (enough to marinate a 3-pound chicken or roast)

	CALORIES	SODIUM
Per serving when dish serves 4:	33	4
With shallots	34.5	4

Yogurt Marinade (10 minutes)

¼ cup low-fat plain yogurt
2 tablespoons apple cider vinegar
1 tablespoon frozen orange juice concentrate (no sugar added)
½ teaspoon Worcestershire sauce
2 teaspoons Italian olive oil

1 tablespoon minced shallot
1 tablespoon Indian Spice Mix (page 000)
½ teaspoon grated lemon rind
2 tablespoons minced fresh parsley or dill

1. Combine all ingredients in a jar.

2. Shake well to blend.

YIELD: About ⅔ cup

	CALORIES	SODIUM
Per serving when dish serves 4:	49	17.5
With dill	No appreciable difference	

Toppings

Fastest Recipes

Whipped Orange Topping (10 minutes)

Use electric mixer

⅓ cup cold evaporated milk
1 tablespoon partially frozen orange juice concentrate (no sugar added)

1 1-gram packet Equal
¼ teaspoon ground cinnamon

1. Pour milk into mixing bowl. Place bowl and whipping utensils in freezer, making certain that bottom of bowl is in contact with metal of freezing compartment. Chill until frozen.

2. In cup, combine orange juice concentrate with Equal, stirring to dissolve. Pour into frozen milk. Sprinkle with cinnamon. Whip on high speed (large whisklike beaters do the most efficient job) until stiff. Serve at once.

YIELD: Serves 6

	CALORIES	SODIUM
Per serving:	30	16.5

Peanut Butter—Pineapple Topping (10 minutes)

Use food blender

⅔ cup drained pineapple chunks packed in unsweetened pineapple juice
3 tablespoons cold peanut butter (no salt added)

2 tablespoons part-skim ricotta cheese

1. Combine all ingredients in blender. Blend until smooth (about 1 minute).

2. Serve at room temperature or chilled.

YIELD: Scant cup

SERVING SUGGESTIONS: Wonderful over puddings, freshly cut fruit, gelatin desserts, and salad greens, or served as a dip.

	CALORIES	SODIUM
Per tablespoon:	62	5

Creamy Yogurt Topping (10 minutes)

3   tablespoons part-skim ricotta cheese
5   tablespoons low-fat plain yogurt
¼   teaspoon each ground cinnamon and freshly grated nutmeg

1   teaspoon finely grated orange rind (preferably from navel orange)
1   1-gram packet Equal

1. Put cheese through sieve or fine strainer into small bowl. Stir in yogurt, spices, and orange rind.

2. Spoon 1 tablespoon mixture into cup. Add Equal and stir to dissolve. Then add to balance of mixture and stir to blend.

YIELD: ⅔ cup

VARIATION: If you're not too calorie conscious, substitute 2 teaspoons honey for Equal. Try it both ways.

	CALORIES	SODIUM
Per tablespoon:	11.5	5.5
With honey	15	5.5

Stock

Faster Recipe

Delicious Chicken Stock (15 minutes)

Use pressure cooker, fine meshed strainer, and cotton cheesecloth

1   3-pound broiling chicken with giblets (excluding liver), skinned, and cut into eighths, well trimmed
1   large onion, coarsely chopped
1   large sweet green pepper, seeded and coarsely chopped
3   large cloves garlic, coarsely chopped
1   medium carrot, scrubbed and thinly sliced

½   cup coarsely chopped celery
¼   cup peeled and diced yellow turnip
1   teaspoon ground ginger
½   teaspoon each dried thyme leaves and savory, crushed
5   cups water
1   cup dry vermouth
    Large bouquet garni (2 sprigs parsley, 1 bay leaf tied together with white thread)

1. Combine all ingredients in uncovered pressure cooker, pushing solids into liquid. Bring to a boil. Cool, uncovered, over medium heat for 5 minutes. Remove from heat. Skim off scum that rises to top.

2. Return pot to heat. Close cover securely. Place regulator on vent pipe and cook for 25 minutes, with pressure regulator rocking slowly. Remove from heat. Let pressure drop of its own accord. Remove whole pieces of chicken and giblets for salad or sandwiches. (Chicken will be very tender.)

3. Place fine meshed strainer over bowl. Pour stock and solids into strainer, pressing to extract juices. Then strain juices through washed cotton cheesecloth. Transfer to freeze-proof containers. Cover tightly and refrigerate overnight or until jelled. Cut away hardened fat that rises to top. Stock is now ready to use.

YIELD: About 3½ cups

ALTERNATE COOKING METHOD: Combine all ingredients in large stainless-steel pot or waterless cooker. Bring to boil. Turn heat down to simmering and cook, uncovered, for 5 minutes, removing scum that rises to top. Cover partially and simmer for 1½ hours, or up to 2½ hours for stronger-tasting stock.

	CALORIES	SODIUM
Per tablespoon:	1.5	6

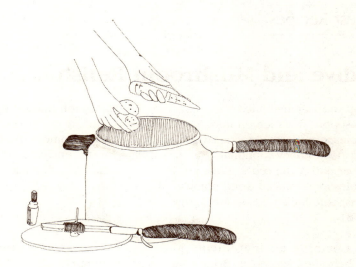

Condiments and Hors d'Oeuvres

Conventional condiments and hors d'oeuvres are appetite stimulants. Mine aren't. My hors d'oeuvres are gentle bridges to a meal. My condiments are flavor enhancers. Both are interesting, different, exciting adventures in the joy of eating—without overeating.

Condiments

Fastest Recipes

Endive and Mushroom Relish (10 minutes)

¼ cup fresh orange juice
2 teaspoons fresh lemon juice
2 tablespoons tarragon vinegar
1 teaspoon honey (optional)
2 tablespoons minced shallots, or 1 tablespoon minced dried onions
1 teaspoon Indian Spice Mix (page 178)

1 tablespoon minced parsley
¼ pound fresh mushrooms, washed, dried, trimmed, and thickly sliced
½ pound endives, trimmed and sliced ½-inch thick

1. Combine all ingredients in heavy-bottomed saucepan. Bring to a boil. Reduce heat to simmering. Partially cover and simmer for 5 minutes. Uncover and let cool.

2. Transfer to a glass jar. Serve at room temperature or chilled.

YIELD: 1½ cups

NOTE: Endives are also known as chicory, witloof, Belgian or French endives.

	CALORIES	SODIUM
Per tablespoon:	10	2.5
With honey	11	2.5
With minced onions	No appreciable difference	

Quick Mixed Fruit Chutney (10 minutes)

1   large crisp sweet apple, cored, peeled, and coarsely chopped
½   cup each fresh cranberries and crushed pineapple (no sugar added)
½   teaspoon fresh lemon juice
3   tablespoons sweet Madeira wine (Malmsey)

2   tablespoons frozen orange juice concentrate (no sugar added)
½   teaspoon ground cinnamon
⅛   teaspoon ground cloves
1   1-gram packet Equal, or 1 teaspoon honey

1. Combine all ingredients except sweetener in heavy-bottomed saucepan. Bring to a boil. Reduce heat to simmering. Cover and simmer for 20 minutes.

2. Uncover and let cool for 5 minutes. Mixture will be thick. Stir in sweetener.

3. Transfer to a glass jar. Tightly cover and chill before serving.

YIELD: 1 cup

	CALORIES	SODIUM
Per tablespoon:	26	.5
With honey	27.5	.5

Hors d'Oeuvres

Faster Recipes

Hot Stuffed Mushrooms (15 minutes)

Preheat oven to 375°F
Use food processor
Use iron skillet

16 medium snow-white fresh mushrooms (1 pound), rinsed, well dried, and trimmed
1 small onion, cut into ½-inch chunks
1 clove garlic, halved
8 large parsley flowerets, rinsed and well dried

1 slice Mixed Wheat Bread (page 173) or good quality commercial whole-wheat bread, toasted, torn into pieces
1 tablespoon each sweet Madeira wine (Malmsey) and pineapple juice (no sugar added)
2 tablespoons grated part-skim mozzarella cheese
2 teaspoons Italian olive oil

1. Fit food processor with steel blade. Remove stems from mushroom caps, and cut in half. Place in processor work bowl. Add onion, garlic, parsley, bread, Madeira, and pineapple juice. Process on/off 4 or 5 times until evenly minced.

2. Stuff mushroom caps, pushing mixture gently into cavity, taking care not to break caps. Sprinkle with cheese, pressing into filling.

3. Spread oil across large well-seasoned iron skillet. Arrange mushrooms in skillet and sauté without moving over medium heat for 2 minutes. Gently loosen from skillet with spatula. Place skillet in preheated oven, uncovered, and bake for 9 to 10 minutes. Finished mushrooms should retain shape and cheese should be completely melted. Serve at once.

YIELD: 16 mushrooms

	CALORIES	SODIUM
Per mushroom:	22.5	10
With commercial whole-wheat bread	22.5	18.5

Broccoli Dip (15 minutes)

Use food processor (optional)

1¼ cups broccoli flowerets (including 1 inch of stem)
¼ cup part-skim ricotta cheese
1 teaspoon finely grated orange rind
½ teaspoon curry powder (no salt or pepper added)

1 teaspoon tomato paste (no salt added)
4 dashes ground red (cayenne) pepper
½ teaspoon each fresh lemon juice and Italian olive oil
2 tablespoons low-fat plain yogurt

1. Set saucepan of water over high heat to boil. While water is heating, peel back thick skin from stem of broccoli. Drop into boiling water. Cook for exactly 8 minutes. Pour into colander. Cool under cold running water for 30 seconds. Drain and coarsely chop. (Or process on/off 3 times in food processor.) Transfer to bowl.

2. Add ricotta cheese, orange rind, and curry powder. Blend with fork.

3. In cup, combine tomato paste, ground red pepper, lemon juice, and oil. Then stir in yogurt. Fold into broccoli mixture. Serve at room temperature.

YIELD: ⅔ cup

	CALORIES	SODIUM
Per tablespoon:	22.5	3.5

Surprise Chicken Balls (15 minutes)

Use food processor

Use nonstick skillet

1 ¾-pound boned and skinned chicken breast, cut into 1-inch chunks
1 small rib celery, sliced
2 large shallots, quartered
2 large cloves garlic, halved
¼ cup rinsed and well-dried parsley flowerets
1 teaspoon Barbeque Spice Mix (page 178)

½ egg (use ½ each yolk and white)
1 teaspoon dry sherry
1 teaspoon prepared Dijon mustard (no salt added)
1 tablespoon low-fat plain yogurt
2 teaspoons Italian olive oil
Juice of ½ lemon

1. Fit food processor with steel blade. In work bowl combine first 6 ingredients. Process 8 to 10 seconds. Mixture should not be totally pureed. Turn into bowl.

2. In work bowl combine egg with sherry and mustard. Process on/off twice. Pour into chicken mixture and blend. Then stir in yogurt. Cover and chill in freezer for 5 minutes. With moistened hands, shape into 22 balls.

3. Spread oil across large nonstick skillet. Heat until quite hot. Add balls, pressing to ½-inch thickness. Sauté for 2 minutes on each side. Turn twice more sautéing each side for 30 seconds. Remove from heat. Sprinkle with lemon juice. Gently shake balls around skillet.

4. Arrange on hot serving dish. Pierce with cocktail picks, and serve at once.

YIELD: 22 balls

	CALORIES	SODIUM
Per ball:	25	15.5

Delicate Shrimp Hors d'Oeuvres (15 minutes)

This is another creation of Shirley Glasner, whose superlative recipe for Golden Chicken Legs appears on page 43.

Use nonstick skillet

1 tablespoon corn oil
3 large cloves garlic, peeled and sliced
¾ pound large unshelled shrimp (shelled and deveined)

⅓ cup dry sherry
2 teaspoons fresh lemon juice
1 tablespoon minced parsley

1. Heat oil in large nonstick skillet over medium heat. Add garlic and sauté, stirring often, until browned (about 3 minutes). Remove garlic with slotted spoon and discard.

2. Dry shrimp well on paper toweling. Add to hot skillet. Sauté on both sides until pink, opaque, and slightly brown around edges (about 4 minutes).

3. Pour sherry over shrimp and continue to cook over slightly higher heat, stirring and turning until sauce is reduced and syrupy (about 3 minutes). Sprinkle with lemon juice. Stir.

4. Transfer to hot serving plate. Sprinkle with parsley, pierce with cocktail picks, and serve at once.

YIELD: Serves 4

VARIATIONS:

1. In step 2, sprinkle and rub shrimp with 1½ teaspoons any of my spice mixes (pages 177—178).

2. Recipe may be served as main course for 2. Serve shrimp over just-cooked rice (allowing ⅓ cup per portion). The small amount of sauce is delectable.

	CALORIES	SODIUM
Per serving:	95	87
With spice mixes	No appreciable difference	
With rice as main dish	227.5	174.5

Mushroom and Liver Pâté (15 minutes)

Use food processor (optional)

¾ cup Delicious Chicken Stock (page 162)

1 envelope unflavored gelatin

½ pound calves liver, cut into 1-inch pieces

¼ pound snow-white fresh mushrooms, washed, dried, trimmed, and sliced

1 teaspoon Indian Spice Mix (page 178)

⅓ cup sweet Madeira wine (Malmsey)

3 tablespoons minced dried onions

⅓ cup tightly packed parsley flowerets, washed and well dried

2 hard-cooked eggs (use 1 egg yolk, 2 egg whites)

2 tablespoons sweet unsalted margarine-butter blend (page 182) or sweet unsalted corn oil margarine

2 tablespoons coarsely chopped unsalted pistachio nuts

1 whole pimento, drained, cut into ⅜-inch strips

1. Place ¼ cup cold stock in dessert cup. Sprinkle with gelatin to soften. Set aside.

2. In heavy-bottomed stainless-steel or enameled saucepan, combine balance of stock, liver, mushrooms, Indian Spice Mix, Madeira, and dried onions. Bring to a boil. Reduce heat to simmering. Partially cover and simmer for 8 minutes.

3. Pour some hot liquid from saucepan into softened gelatin, stirring to dissolve completely. Set aside.

4. Pour balance of ingredients in saucepan into food processor that has

been fitted with steel blade (see Note). Add parsley flowerets, eggs, and margarine-butter blend. Process until smooth (about 1 minute). Turn into bowl.

5. Stir in dissolved gelatin mixture, blending well.

6. Rinse out small loaf pan (7⅜" × 3⅜" × 2¼" or decorative mold of equivalent volume). Sprinkle with pistachio nuts. Garnish with pimento strips in a decorative pattern. Cover with plastic wrap. Chill until firm (about 1½ hours).

YIELD: Serves 6

NOTE: Step 4 may be completed by hand. Here's how: Drain solids, pouring cooking liquid into bowl. Chop solids and parsley with sharp knife as fine as possible. Mash eggs with margarine-butter blend. Then transfer chopped and mashed ingredients to bowl with reserved cooking liquid. Continue with balance of recipe.

	CALORIES	SODIUM
Per serving:	130	39
With margarine	No appreciable difference	

Veal Cocktail Balls (15 minutes)

Use iron skillet

½ pound each lean ground veal and pork
½ teaspoon each ground sage, dried rosemary leaves, crushed, and ground cinnamon
6 dashes ground red (cayenne) pepper
2 slices Mixed Wheat Bread (page 173) or thin-sliced good quality commercial whole-wheat bread

¾ cup dry red wine
2 teaspoons tomato paste (no salt added)
1 tablespoon peanut oil
2 tablespoons each minced shallots and sweet red pepper
⅓ cup apple juice (no sugar added)

1. In bowl, combine and blend first three listed ingredients.

2. Tear bread (including crust) into small pieces. Place in small bowl. Combine ¼ cup wine with tomato paste, beating with fork to blend. Pour over bread, breaking up pieces with fork. Let stand for 1 minute. Stir into meat mixture. Shape into 24 compact balls.

3. Heat oil in well-seasoned iron skillet until hot. Spread shallots and sweet red pepper across skillet. Sauté for 30 seconds. Lay veal balls on minced mixture and brown over medium-high heat, turning from time to time, and regulating heat, if necessary, so that meat doesn't stick (about 4 minutes).

4. Add remaining ½ cup of wine and apple juice, turning balls several times to coat. Bring to simmering point. Cover and simmer for 10 minutes, stirring once midway.

5. Uncover. Raise heat. Cook for 3 minutes, turning balls often. Sauce will reduce by half and cling to meat. Remove from heat. Cover and let stand for 2 to 3 minutes.

6. Pierce with colorful cocktail picks and serve immediately.

YIELD: 24 cocktail balls

	CALORIES	SODIUM
Per ball:	38	16.5
With commercial whole-wheat bread	38	22

Breads

Mixed Wheat Bread Crumbs (10 minutes)

As elegant as the bread from which it's made (see page 173).

Preheat oven to 425°F
Use food blender

1. Cut 6 ⅜-inch slices Mixed Wheat Bread into ½-inch cubes. Spread on cookie sheet and bake in preheated oven for 8 to 10 minutes, turning once with spatula. Let cool.

2. Transfer to food blender and blend on high speed for 1 minute.
3. Pour into a jar. Cover tightly and store in refrigerator.

YIELD: About 1 cup

	CALORIES	SODIUM
Per tablespoon:	23	1

Delicate Textured Loaf (15 minutes)

Taste it, and say good-bye to store-bought bread forever. It makes light and lovely crumbs (instructions above), does marvels for stuffings and sandwiches, and converts to never-before-tasted deliciousness in French toast (page 119). Best of all, just one slice will stick to your ribs until your next meal—really!

Use food processor

¼ cup warm water (105° to 115°F)

1 teaspoon honey

1 tablespoon dry yeast, or 1 premeasured package

2½-2¾ cups unbleached flour

⅓ cup medium rye flour

2 teaspoons peanut or corn oil, plus ¼ teaspoon for rising bowl

2 tablespoons each nonfat dry milk and low-fat plain yogurt

1 teaspoon finely grated orange rind (preferably from navel orange)

1½ teaspoons aniseed, crushed

⅓ cup each water and apple juice (no sugar added)

½ teaspoon sweet unsalted corn oil margarine for waxed paper and loaf pan

1 egg white mixed with 1 tablespoon water

1 tablespoon poppy seed or unhulled sesame seed

1. In cup, combine water, honey, and yeast. Beat with fork to blend. Let stand while balance of ingredients are assembled. Mixture will puff up.

2. Fit processor with steel blade. In work bowl combine 2½ cups unbleached flour, all of rye flour, oil, dry milk, yogurt, orange rind, and aniseed. Process on/off 4 to 5 times.

3. Pour yeast mixture over flour mixture. Process on/off 4 times.

4. Heat water and apple juice to lukewarm—not hot. With processor running, dribble into work bowl. Continue to process until dough forms into ball and rotates around bowl several times. Dough will be sticky. Stop machine. Let dough rest for 2 minutes.

5. Turn processor on. Sprinkle ⅛ cup unbleached flour through feed tube. Dough will form into ball and rotate around bowl. Use balance of flour (⅛ cup) if ball is still very sticky. Total processing time should not exceed 15 seconds.

6. Turn onto board and knead until smooth and pliable and no longer sticky (1½ to 2 minutes). Shape into ball. Drop into fairly straight-sided lightly oiled bowl, turning to coat. Cover tightly with plastic wrap and let rise in warm place (70° to 80°F) until more than double in bulk (about 1¼ hours).

7. Punch dough down. Knead for 1 minute. Shape into loaf. Place in lightly greased 9-inch loaf pan. Cover with sheet of waxed paper which has been lightly greased with margarine. Let rise until well above sides of pan (about 1 hour). Carefully remove waxed paper. Preheat oven to 375°F.

8. Brush lightly with egg white mixture. Sprinkle with aniseed. Bake in center section of oven for 40 to 45 minutes. Test for doneness by tapping bottom of loaf with knuckles. If you hear a hollow sound, your loaf is fully baked. If not, place back in oven directly on rack and bake an additional 4 to 5 minutes. Place on rack and cool completely before slicing.

YIELD: 1 loaf; 24 ⅜-inch slices

BREAD CRUMBS: Follow directions for Mixed Wheat Bread Crumbs (page 171); 5½ slices yield about 1 cup.

	CALORIES	SODIUM
Per slice:	67	8
With sesame seed	No appreciable difference	
Per tablespoon bread crumbs:	23	3

Mixed Wheat Bread (15 minutes)

The nutlike crunchiness of the burnished crust contrasts exquisitely with the slightly sweet, cakelike-textured center. An elegant bread. And it makes the best toast ever.

Use food processor

1 tablespoon dry yeast, or 1 pre-measured package
1 teaspoon honey
¼ cup warm water (105° to 115°F)
2½ cups unbleached flour
⅓ cup stone-ground whole-wheat flour
2 tablespoons The Healthy Sweetener (page 182)
1 teaspoon aniseed, crushed
½ teaspoon each ground cinnamon and cardamom

1 teaspoon finely grated orange rind (preferably from navel orange)
1 tablespoon peanut oil, plus ¼ teaspoon for rising bowl
⅓ cup nonfat liquid milk
½ cup apple juice (no sugar added)
½ teaspoon sweet unsalted corn oil margarine for pan and waxed paper

1. In cup, combine yeast, honey, and water. Beat with fork to blend. Let stand while balance of ingredients are assembled. Mixture will puff up.

2. Fit processor with steel blade. Combine all but 1 tablespoon unbleached flour, all whole-wheat flour, The Healthy Sweetener, aniseed, spices, orange rind, and 1 tablespoon oil in work bowl. Turn processor on/off 4 times to blend.

3. Pour yeast mixture over dry ingredients. Process on/off 3 times.

4. Heat nonfat milk and apple juice until warm (105° to 115°F). With processor on, dribble three fourths of liquid through feed tube. Dough will

form into ball as soon as liquid is absorbed. Process for 10 seconds, dribbling in more liquid, if necessary. Turn off processor. Let dough stand for 2 minutes.

5. With processor on, pour balance of apple juice—milk mixture through feed tube. Stop machine after dough cleans side of bowl. Turn dough onto board that is sprinkled with balance of flour (1 tablespoon) and knead for 1 minute by hand. Dough will be smooth and very soft in texture.

6. Form into ball. Place in fairly straight-sided, lightly oiled bowl, turning to coat. Cover tightly with plastic wrap and let rise in a warm place (70°

to 80°F) until more than doubled in bulk (about 1¼ hours).

7. Punch dough down. Knead for 1 minute. Shape into loaf. Place in lightly greased 9-inch loaf pan. Cover with sheet of waxed paper that has been lightly greased with margarine. Let rise until well above sides of pan (about 1 hour). Carefully remove waxed paper. Preheat oven to 375°F.

8. Bake in center section of oven for 40 to 45 minutes. Remove from pan. Finished loaf should produce a hollow sound when tapped with knuckles. Let cool completely on rack before slicing.

YIELD: 1 loaf; 24 ⅜-inch slices.

BREAD CRUMBS: See page 171.

	CALORIES	SODIUM
Per slice:	61	2.5

Fast Recipes

Onion Rye Loaves (20 minutes)

So popular has home bread-making become in the last several years that the dough hook is now standard equipment on mixing machines. So use your dough hook (unless you prefer the joy of kneading by hand) to prepare these examples of perfect homemade loaves. Thin-sliced, they're superlative as-is, with all kinds of sandwich fillings, and as toast (*that's* when the onion-y flavor peaks). And crumbed (fine or soft), they convert to a wonder ingredient in breading and stuffings.

Use electric mixer with dough hook

2	tablespoons dry yeast, or 2 premeasured packages	5	teaspoons peanut oil
2	cups medium rye flour	1	tablespoon honey
3-3¼	cups unbleached flour	1	tablespoon coarsely grated orange rind (preferably from navel orange)
¼	cup unprocessed bran		
2	tablespoons minced dried onions		
1½	teaspoons each caraway seed and aniseed, partially crushed	½	teaspoon sweet unsalted corn oil margarine
1	cup each buttermilk (no salt added) and apple juice (no sugar added)	1	egg white, beaten with 1 tablespoon of water

1. In large mixing bowl, combine and stir yeast, 1 cup rye flour, 1 cup unbleached flour, bran, onions, and seeds.

2. In heavy-bottomed saucepan combine and slowly heat buttermilk, apple juice, 4½ teaspoons oil, honey, and orange rind until warm (105° to 115°F). Pour over dry ingredients and beat with wooden spoon for 2 minutes, or use electric mixer at medium speed for 1 minute. Cover tightly with plastic wrap and let stand for 10 minutes.

3. Stir down. Add balance of rye flour (1 cup) and 1 cup unbleached flour. Beat until well blended. Add 1 cup of remaining unbleached flour, ¼ cup at a time, beating after each addition. When dough becomes too difficult to handle with wooden spoon, turn onto lightly floured board (or use dough hook) and knead until smooth and elastic, using balance of flour (¼ cup), if necessary, to make a smooth, elastic, nonsticky dough.

4. Shape into a ball. Drop into fairly straight-sided bowl that has been lightly rubbed with ½ teaspoon remaining peanut oil. Cover tightly with plastic wrap and let rise at room temperature (70° to 80°F) until double in bulk (about 1¼ hours).

5. Punch dough down. Turn onto board and knead briefly. Shape into ball. Divide in half. Shape each piece into loaf. Place in 2 margarine-greased small loaf pans (7⅜" × 3⅝" × 2¼"). Cover with sheet of margarine-greased waxed paper. Let rise until well above sides of pans. Preheat oven to 375°F.

6. Gently brush loaves with egg white mixture. Bake in center section of oven for 45 to 50 minutes, removing from pans and testing loaves for doneness by thumping knuckles. A hollow sound indicates the loaves are done.

7. Remove bread from pans. Let cool on rack completely before slicing.

YIELD: 2 loaves; 20 high ⅜-inch slices

BREAD CRUMBS: Follow directions for Mixed Wheat Bread Crumbs (page 171); 4½ slices yield about 1 cup.

	CALORIES	SODIUM
Per slice:	70	4.3
Per tablespoon bread crumbs:	20	1

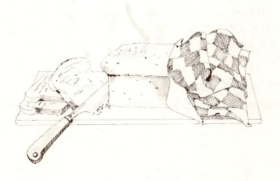

Orange Rye Loaves (20 minutes)

Use electric mixer with dough hook

2	tablespoons dry yeast, or 2 premeasured packages
1	cup medium rye flour
4¼-4½	cups unbleached flour
1	teaspoon each ground coriander and ground cardamom
1	tablespoon caraway seed, partially crushed
2	cups nonfat liquid milk
1	tablespoon sweet unsalted margarine-butter blend

	(page 182) or sweet unsalted corn oil margarine, plus 1 teaspoon for pans and waxed paper
3	tablespoons low-fat plain yogurt
2	tablespoons frozen orange juice concentrate (no sugar added)
½	teaspoon peanut oil
1	egg white mixed with 1 teaspoon water

1. In large mixing bowl, combine yeast, rye flour, 2 cups unbleached flour, spices, and caraway seed.

2. Heat nonfat milk and margarine-butter blend until warm (105° to 115°F). Pour over dry ingredients and beat on medium speed for 2 minutes. Cover tightly with plastic wrap and let stand for 10 minutes.

3. While batter is standing, in cup, combine and blend yogurt with orange juice concentrate. Stir yeast mixture down. With wooden spoon, cut yogurt mixture into batter until absorbed. Then beat with dough hook, adding all but ¼ cup of balance of unbleached flour (2¼ cups), until dough forms into ball and cleans bowl. If dough remains sticky, add the ¼ cup remaining flour. Knead with dough hook for 3 minutes. Dough is fully kneaded when it's soft, satiny, and nonsticky to handle.

4. Shape into ball. Drop into fairly straight-sided bowl that has been rubbed with peanut oil. Cover tightly with plastic wrap and let rise at room temperature (70° to 80°F) until double in bulk (about 1¼ hours).

5. Punch dough down. Turn onto board and knead briefly. Divide into 3 equal pieces. Shape each piece into loaf. Place in 3 lightly greased small loaf pans (7⅜" × 3⅝" × 2¼"). Cover with sheet of greased waxed paper. Let rise until above sides of pans (about 1¼ hours). Preheat oven to 425°F.

6. Gently brush loaves with egg white mixture. Bake in center section of oven for 10 minutes. Reduce heat to 375°F and bake for 30 to 35 minutes. Finished loaves should be well browned and crispy all over.

7. Remove bread from pans. Let cool on rack completely before slicing.

YIELD: 3 loaves; 20 ⅜-inch slices.

BREAD CRUMBS: Follow directions for Mixed Wheat Bread Crumbs (page 171); 6 slices yield about 1 cup.

	CALORIES	SODIUM
Per slice:	60	5.5
Per tablespoon bread crumbs:	17	.5

Ready-Access Foods

Keep handy these three original spice mixes; minced parsley, shallots or onions; and that wonder of French cookery, duxelles—and you're ready at the drop of a hint to create sauces, stuffings, soups, vegetables, and a whole gamut of entrées.

Fastest Recipes

Herb 'n Spice Mix (10 minutes)

1½ teaspoons dried thyme leaves, crushed
3 tablespoons dried tarragon leaves, crushed, or 2 tablespoons dried tarragon leaves and 1 tablespoon dried savory leaves, crushed

4½ teaspoons ground ginger
½ teaspoon ground red (cayenne) pepper
1 tablespoon onion powder
1 teaspoon freshly grated nutmeg

1. Combine all ingredients in bowl, stirring well to blend. Transfer to a jar.

2. Store, tightly closed, in cool dry place.

YIELD: ½ cup

NOTE: Stir before using; dried herbs tend to settle to bottom of mixture.

	CALORIES	SODIUM
Per teaspoon:	5.5	1

Barbeque Spice Mix (10 minutes)

2 teaspoons onion powder
1 teaspoon ground ginger
2 teaspoons dried rosemary leaves, crushed
1½ teaspoons each ground marjoram and dried oregano leaves, crushed

2 tablespoons curry powder (no salt or pepper added)
3 tablespoons chili con carne seasoning (no salt or pepper added)
¼ teaspoon ground red (cayenne) pepper

1. Combine all ingredients in bowl, stirring well to blend. Transfer to a jar.

2. Store, tightly closed, in cool dry place.

YIELD: Scant ½ cup

	CALORIES	SODIUM
Per teaspoon:	6.5	1

Indian Spice Mix (10 minutes)

3 tablespoons each ground coriander and ginger
4½ teaspoons ground cumin
¾ teaspoon ground red (cayenne) pepper

¾ teaspoon each ground cardamom and freshly grated nutmeg
1½ teaspoons dried savory leaves, crushed

1. Combine all ingredients in bowl, stirring well to blend. Transfer to a jar.

2. Store, tightly closed, in cool dry place.

YIELD: About ½ cup

	CALORIES	SODIUM
Per teaspoon:	5	1.5

Ready Parsley (10 minutes)

Use food processor or sharp knife

Fresh parsley

1. Wash flowerets from bunch(es) of parsley under cold running water. Lay between double thickness of paper toweling and press dry.

2. Mince in work bowl of food processor that has been fitted with steel blade by turning on/off two to

three times. Do not overprocess. (Or chop finely by hand with sharp knife.)

3. Spread parsley across aluminum-lined baking sheet. Cover tightly with another sheet of foil and freeze.

4. When frozen, uncover and fold over aluminum foil to loosen parsley. Store in freezer in freezeproof container. Use as needed.

YIELD: As much as you want to make

NOTE: When using sharp knife add 2 to 3 minutes chopping time.

	CALORIES	SODIUM
Per tablespoon:	2	2

Ready Shallots or Onions (10 minutes)

Use food processor or sharp knife
½ pound shallots or onions

1. Peel shallots or onions. Mince in food processor by cutting shallots in half or cutting onions into 1-inch pieces. Then process in work bowl of food processor that has been fitted with steel blade by turning on/off 2 or 3 times. Take care that ingredient(s) are not reduced to liquid. (You can also mince by hand. Add 3 to 4 minutes chopping time.)

2. Spread across aluminum-lined baking sheet. Cover tightly with another sheet of foil and freeze.

3. When frozen, uncover, and fold over aluminum foil to loosen shallots or onions. Store in freezeproof container. Use as needed.

YIELD: About 1 cup

	CALORIES	SODIUM
Shallots, per tablespoon:	7	1
Onion, per tablespoon:	4	1

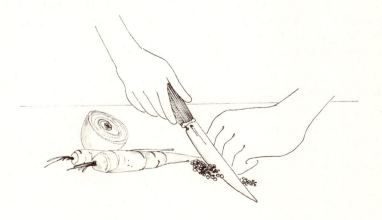

Faster Recipe

Ready Duxelles (15 minutes)

Use food processor or sharp knife
Use iron skillet

8   medium shallots, or 4 medium shallots and ½ small onion
2   cloves garlic
3   parsley flowerets
1   pound snow white mushrooms, washed, dried, and trimmed
4   teaspoons each peanut oil and sweet unsalted margarine-butter blend (page 182)

½   teaspoon each dried tarragon and chervil leaves, crumbled
⅛   teaspoon ground red (cayenne) pepper
¼   cup sweet Madeira wine (Malmsey)

1. Peel shallots (or shallots and onion) and garlic. Mince by hand, or cut shallots in half (onion into 1-inch pieces) and process in work bowl of food processor, fitted with steel blade, by turning on/off 2 or 3 times. Take care that ingredient(s) are not reduced to liquid. Transfer to measuring cup. There should be a little more than ½ cup.

2. Mince parsley and mushrooms by hand or mince in food processor by breaking apart parsley flowerets and quartering mushrooms. Then process in work bowl of food processor by turning on/off 2 or 3 times. Take care that ingredients are not reduced to liquid. Transfer to dish.

3. Heat oil and margarine-butter blend in well-seasoned iron skillet until hot but not browned. Sauté shallots (or shallots and onion) and garlic until wilted, stirring constantly.

4. Add mushroom mixture. Reduce to medium heat. Sprinkle with tarragon, chervil, and ground red pepper. Continue sautéing until all liquid evaporates.

5. Add Madeira. Simmer gently, stirring often, until all liquid evaporates. Let cool.

6. Transfer to freezeproof container. Close tightly and freeze.

YIELD: About 1½ cups

	CALORIES	SODIUM
Per tablespoon:	22	3.5
With minced shallots and onions		
	No appreciable difference	

Bare Basics

To slash your kitchen-time keep these healthful ingredients in your kitchen all the time.

BREADS AND RELATED PRODUCTS: baking powder; breads; unseasoned bread crumbs; unbleached, enriched flour.

DAIRY PRODUCTS: eggs, evaporated skim and whole milk; nonfat milk; sweet, unsalted corn oil margarine; sweet-unsalted margarine-butter blend; part-skim mozzarella cheese; part-skim ricotta cheese; low-fat plain yogurt.

FRUITS: lemons, limes, oranges, canned pineapple chunks packed in unsweetened pineapple juice; raisins.

JUICES: apple juice; frozen fruit juice concentrates; pineapple juice—all without added sugar.

READY-ACCESS FOODS: See pages 177–179.

SPICES AND VINEGARS: apple cider vinegar; tarragon vinegar; wine vinegar; a wide variety of spices and dried herbs (see recipes for spice mixes, pages 177–178).

SWEETENERS: Equal or another aspartame product; raw, unfiltered honey.

VEGETABLES AND RELATED PRODUCTS: garlic; dried legumes; mushrooms; onions; parsley; shallots; sweet peppers; canned tomatoes; tomatoes; tomato paste; tomato purée (all tomato products with no salt added).

WINES: Madeira (Malmsey); Marsala; dry red and white wine; Vermouth.

Sources of Some Favored Ingredients

1. Tomato puree, low-sodium prepared Dijon mustard, unsweetened jellies, bulgur, natural dried fruits, date sugar (also called date powder), unshelled sesame seed, whole kasha, and nonfat dry milk are available in health food stores. Bulgur is also available by mail from Sovex, Inc., Box 310, Collegedale, TN 37315. Date powder is also available by mail from Sunshine Valley, P.O. Box 5517, Sherman Oaks, CA 91413.

2. The Healthy Sweetener is generally available in supermarkets and specialty stores or by mail from Shaffer Clarke & Company, 1445 East Putnam Avenue, Old Greenwich, CT 06870.

3. Bottled spices, herbs, juniper berries, arrowroot flour, and margarine-butter blends (such as Country Morning Blend) can be found in supermarkets. Chili con carne seasoning and juniper berries are bottled under the trade name Spice Islands, which is manufactured by Specialty Brands, Inc., San Francisco, CA 94111.

4. Low-sodium tomato juice, tomato paste, canned whole tomatoes, and jarred pimentos are generally available on diet shelves and regular shelves of supermarkets.

5. Evaporated milk is generally available in supermarkets.

6. No-fat Sap Sago cheese (imported by Emmental Cheese Corporation, 175 Clearbrook Road, Elmsford, NY 10523) is available in cheese specialty stores or gourmet shops.

7. Pasta products with no salt added are available in supermarkets.

Index